THE TRUTH ABOUT THE NATIONAL DEBT

The Truth about the National Debt

Five Myths and One Reality

FRANCIS X. CAVANAUGH

Harvard Business School Press
Boston, Massachusetts

336.34

℮

00 99 98 97 96   5 4 3 2 1

Library of Congress Cataloging-in-Publication Data

Cavanaugh, Francis X.

    The truth about the national debt : five myths and one reality /
Francis X. Cavanaugh.

      p.   cm.

    Includes bibliographical references and index.

    ISBN 0-87584-734-X (alk. paper)

    1. Debts, Public—United States.   2. Budget deficits—United
States.   3. Government spending policy—United States.   I. Title.

HJ8119.C38   1996

336.3'4'0973—dc20   96-4074

                                                      CIP

TO
CAROL

CONTENTS

PREFACE

THE HISTORIC CLASH in the winter of 1995–1996 between Congress and the President over balancing the federal budget made the federal debt a front-page story throughout the country. Disagreement over the budget threatened to precipitate a financial crisis as Congress refused to increase the limit on the Treasury Department's authority to borrow. Without an increase in that debt limit, the Treasury would be unable to raise the money needed to meet its financial obligations, including interest due on Treasury's outstanding debt. For the first time in its history, there was a serious question as to whether the U.S. government would be permitted to pay its bills.

As a long-time "Washington insider" and a veteran of many Treasury Department battles with Congress over the public debt limit, I didn't think much would come of this one. My initial reaction to the threats that the Treasury might be forced to default on its obligations was, "Ho hum, just a lot of political talk. The most they'll ever do is shut down a few minor government activities for a couple of days, probably over a weekend, and make the Treasury squirm for a few weeks while they delay action on the needed legislation to increase the public debt limit."

Was I ever wrong! The past was no longer prologue. Washington reached new heights of fiscal folly. Significant parts of the government were shut down not for two days but for three weeks. Congress barred the Treasury from borrowing for so long that Moody's Investor Service, a major bond-rating agency, took the unprecedented action of placing part of the U.S. Treasury debt on CreditWatch for possible downgrade—not because of any weakness in the U.S. economy, which is the strongest in the world, but because politicians could not find a way to settle their differences. It was that failure of leadership that shocked me into the realization that our ship of state was indeed manned by a ship of fools. Thus, this book.

I was further shocked when my wife told me that her mother and her mother's neighbor, both elderly widows, said they were willing to go without a cost-of-living increase in their modest Social Security incomes to help the President reduce the public debt.

I said to myself, "We have clearly gone too far in frightening people about the national debt." There had been many volunteer efforts, such as bake sales, by school children and other patriotic citizens to raise money to send to the U.S. Treasury to help reduce the debt, but I always viewed them as constructive expressions of our national sense of community. It is an entirely different matter to take a widow's mite—causing little old ladies throughout the country to water down their soup so they can contribute to reducing the federal debt. If there is to be a final Judgment Day, we could get hell for that.

The $5 trillion national debt has also become a seriously divisive issue, as evidenced by the growing resentment expressed by young people, especially those in their twenties, about the burden of the debt being passed on to them by their seemingly irresponsible elders. Indeed, the national debt burden has become a major concern of "twentysomething" groups, such as the Third Millennium and Lead . . . or Leave, the organization that picketed the Washington head-quarters of the American Association of Retired Persons in 1993. This resentment has been deepened by the army of business and political leaders who grossly exaggerate the "future debt burden" in their speeches on college campuses and on the talk-show circuit.

I spent thirty-two years as an economist and federal debt manager in the U.S. Treasury Department, but I have never seen as much public concern over the national debt as there is today. Voluntary contributions to the Treasury's "debt reduction fund" soared to more than $21 million in fiscal year 1994, almost as much as the $25 million total of all previous contributions over the thirty-three-year period since the fund was established in 1961.

Our political leaders continue to point to the federal debt with alarm, but then they do nothing to reduce it. No wonder our young people are fearful about the future! It seems that the federal debt will never be reduced. The debt has increased in every year since 1969 because during each of those years the federal government has had a budget deficit—that is, an excess of expenditures over taxes and other receipts. The annual deficits were financed by the sale of Treasury securities, thereby adding to the federal debt. We have never raised the taxes needed to pay off the World War II debt and probably never will; we just keep rolling it over, refinancing with issues of new Treasury securities to replace the old securities as they come due.

Yet we have become the strongest economy in the world, the only superpower. The prophets of doom and gloom—scaring people about the coming "day of reckoning" or "bankruptcy" of the United States because of the growing national debt—have turned out to be false prophets. They were (and are) dead wrong.

Why, then, do our political leaders continue to sound alarms about the national debt? Do they think that's what the voters want to hear? Do they really believe what they say, but lack what it takes to do something about it? Do they find it politically advantageous to blame their opponents for "shocking" debt increases? Do conservative leaders find scare talk about the debt to be a useful way to frustrate the social program spenders in Congress (while preserving the national defense contracts, agricultural subsidies, and other programs favored by conservatives)? Do liberal leaders find that such scare talk is a useful way to justify tax increases (for more social spending) or cutbacks in defense spending? Have we reached a point where both conservative and liberal presidents can use the American people's common fear of the debt to accomplish their diametrically opposite goals? As I reflect on my service to seven presidents and thirteen secretaries of the Treasury on public-debt management policy issues, I would say that the answer to all of the above questions is yes.

A current example of those scare tactics (by both political parties) is the national debate over the phony issue of reducing the public debt versus maintaining the safety net provided by the Social Security system. I will show that the Social Security financing problem has nothing to do with the national debt.

My book is an effort to set the record straight, to explode the five principal myths about the national debt, and to explain that our biggest fiscal problem is undisciplined government spending, *not* the way we pay for it, whether through debt or taxes. I also propose changes in the federal budget and debt-limit processes that will restore discipline to government spending and public confidence in the management of the government's finances.

My primary purpose is to communicate to young Americans that their inheritance—the greatest economy the world has ever known—is in danger of being diminished not by the national debt but by a failure of political leadership. I would hope to encourage them to question the conventional wisdom about the national debt and to challenge their political leaders to an enlightened discussion of these issues.

ACKNOWLEDGMENTS

I WOULD LIKE TO express my deep appreciation for the invaluable support of Roger W. Mehle, his constant encouragement, patient listening, wise counsel, and exceptional editorial talents.

I am also much indebted to Brian J. Cavanaugh, James W. Sauber, and Charles O. Sethness for their encouragement and for the generous gift of their time and valuable insights at many stages in the development of this book.

There are many others, too numerous to mention, especially my family and my former associates at the U.S. Treasury Department and the Federal Retirement Thrift Investment Board, who contributed in many ways to this effort to communicate with the American people about their national debt.

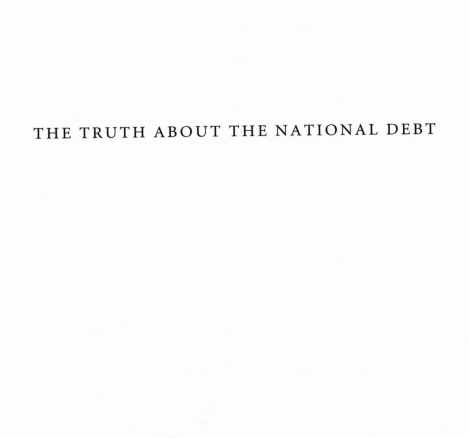

THE TRUTH ABOUT THE NATIONAL DEBT

INTRODUCTION Do We Know Why We Hate the Deficit?

IT USED TO BE a lot easier to name things on which the American people agreed. The old standby icons of Mom, apple pie, and the flag have lost ground to open lifestyles, low-fat desserts, and tolerance for flag burning. What's left?

Ronald Reagan noted one item of apparent universal agreement in 1993: "Every person in this country realizes the serious need to reduce the federal deficit. There is no disagreement on this issue."[1]

That was perhaps a bit of an overstatement by our former president. To reduce its annual budget deficit, the government must raise taxes, lower spending, or do both (based on the economic growth assumptions of both the congressional and administration analysts). But the elected voices of the people are proposing to lower taxes, and it remains to be seen whether their promised cuts in federal spending at the turn of the century will really take place.

Yet it seems fair to say that the federal deficit has achieved at least the status of economic public enemy number one. Economic public enemy number two may be the result of the accumulation of years of federal deficits—the federal debt, a.k.a. the national debt, the government debt, or the public debt.

Economists from time to time point to unemployment, inflation, low productivity, or inequitable distribution of income as the real economic villain, but it is only the deficit that seems to endure over the years as the common enemy the American people love to hate. Why is that? Do we know why we hate the deficit? We need to know, of course, to take the right corrective measures. Or to put it another and perhaps better way, we need to understand the nature of the deficit to avoid taking the wrong corrective measures, such as excessive increases in our taxes or spending cuts in vital government programs.

In that context, I believe that we don't understand the nature of the deficit. I have reached that conclusion because the major reasons for cutting the deficit given by political leaders—reflecting the *vox populi*—do not make sense. They are what I call "the myths of debt and deficits." Like all myths, they are perennial and intuitive, and they carry a resonant message. I list them in the order of their seeming exigence:

- First, federal budget deficits and debt add to the economic burden on future generations; indeed, we are "mortgaging our children's future."
- Second, the sale of large amounts of Treasury securities to finance the annual deficits puts upward pressure on market interest rates and thus "crowds out" private borrowing for worthwhile investments.
- Third, interest payments on the mounting federal debt are becoming an unsustainable burden on the federal budget.
- Fourth, interest on the federal debt is regressive—it is paid largely to wealthy investors from taxes collected from people of just average income.
- Fifth, we are becoming too dependent on foreigners to finance our budget deficits.

All five of these myths have persisted—and flourished—for many years, even though some of them had been thoroughly debated and discredited forty years ago, when I began my career as an economist with the U.S. Treasury Department. At that time the country was concerned about sustaining the post–World War II debt burden (discussed later), which was twice the size of today's. Yet people seem to be more concerned about the debt today than they were then.

In the following chapters I discuss the various common measures of the alleged burden of the national debt (chapter 1), the fallacies of each of the five myths as arguments for reducing the deficit (chapters

2–6), the federal takeover of U.S. credit markets (chapter 7), the alleged impact of the national debt on the financing of the Social Security system (chapter 8), the apparent reasons why political leaders do not tell the truth about the national debt (chapter 9), and, finally, the reality—the real reason (spending control) we should hate the deficit and take corrective action to restore confidence in government and discipline in the federal budget (chapter 10).

1   The Size of the Problem

In MAY 1995, the Budget Committee of the House of Representatives met to approve a resolution to balance the federal budget by the year 2002, the so-called crown jewel of the House Republicans' Contract with America. The chairman of the committee, Republican John Kasich of Ohio, unveiled a large digital "national debt clock" on the wall of the committee hearing room where the TV cameras—and, thereby, the American people—could view with alarm a federal debt figure—nearing $5 trillion—ticking away like a time bomb to blow us all to smithereens. The obvious message was that we need to balance the budget because the public debt is "too big." But how big is too big? How much deficit (or debt) reduction would it take to fix Congressman Kasich's clock?

First, some perspective. Just as the burden of an individual home mortgage has meaning only when compared with the income of the homeowner, the federal deficit and debt numbers are meaningful only in the context of other numbers that reflect our national financial condition.

DEBT/GDP RATIO

The debt statistic perhaps cited most by economists and government officials is the ratio of the net federal debt to the gross domestic product, or GDP. GDP is the value of goods and services produced in the United States each year, and therefore is a measure of our nation's production.[1] The ratio is viewed as a useful measure of the current burden of the debt on our economy or, put another way, of how much of our annual production would be needed to pay off the debt. The federal debt is almost entirely in the form of securities (bills, notes, and bonds) issued by the U.S. Treasury Department.[2] As shown in table 1-1, the net federal debt is the debt held by the public, which is the gross debt less the debt held by the government itself in the Social Security trust funds and other government accounts.

The official explanation for the net federal debt calculation is that debt held by the public is "a better concept than gross federal debt for

Table 1-1 Federal government financing and debt, fiscal year 1995 (billions of dollars)

Financing	
Budget deficit[a]	163.9
Less: Means of financing the deficit other than borrowing from the public[b]	−7.4
Equals: Net increase in federal debt held by the public	171.3
Debt, end of year	
Gross federal debt	4,921.0
Less:	
Debt held by federal trust funds	1,282.4
Social Security (OASDI)	483.2
Federal civilian employees retirement	374.3
Military retirement	126.7
Medicare:	
Hospital insurance	129.5
Supplementary Medical Insurance	13.9
Unemployment	47.9
Transportation	30.4
Veterans life insurance	13.6
Railroad retirement	14.4
Federal employees health benefits	7.8
Foreign military sales	5.5
Other trust funds	35.2
Debt held by other government accounts	35.2[c]
Equals: Net debt held by the public	3,603.4

Source: Office of Management and Budget, Analytical Perspectives, Budget of the United States Government, Fiscal Year 1997 (Washington, D.C.: GPO, 1996), 189, 263–269.

[a]Includes both on-budget and off-budget accounts.
[b]Includes a $16.6 billion decrease in Treasury cash balance and minor changes in other nondebt items.
[c]Includes surface transportation and aviation accounts.

analyzing the effect of the budget on the economy."[3] This accounting treatment is confusing to people who think the Social Security and other government "trust funds" are owned by the beneficiaries of the trusts—they are not. The Treasury securities in the Social Security trust fund, for example, are not held by the Social Security beneficiaries; thus they are not "held by the public." Yet the designation of the Social Security fund as a "trust fund" suggests that the fund is held in trust for the beneficiaries. This confusion has led to considerable debate in Congress as to the investments and proper budgetary treatment of the Social Security trust fund (which I will discuss in chapter 8).

The following statement from President Clinton's budget for fiscal year 1996 makes clear that the Social Security and certain other government "trust funds" are trust funds in name only:

> Whether or not a particular fund is designated as a trust fund is, in many cases, arbitrary. Congress has not followed a systematic rule. For example, the National Service Life Insurance Fund is a trust fund, but the Servicemen's Group Life Insurance Fund is a Federal fund, even though both are financed by fees paid by veterans and both provide life insurance benefits to veterans.
>
> The Federal budget meaning of the term "trust" differs significantly from its private sector usage. In the private sector, the beneficiary of a trust owns the income generated by the trust and usually its assets. A trustee, acting as a fiduciary, manages the trust's assets on behalf of the beneficiary. The trustee is required to follow the stipulations of the trust, which he cannot change unilaterally. In contrast, the Federal Government owns the assets and earnings of Federal trust funds, and it can raise or lower future trust fund collections and payments, or change the purpose for which the collections are used, by changing existing law.[4]

In fact, Congress has made many major changes in Social Security taxes and benefits and is contemplating many more. But I have yet to meet a politician who will stand up and say, "The Social Security fund is not a trust fund."

To make matters more complicated, the government does manage some "true" trust funds (that is, they are like private trust funds), but they are not classified as trust funds for federal budget purposes. These are funds that are invested in Treasury securities held in trust for the exclusive benefit of nonfederal persons. Most notably, the $40 billion Thrift Savings Fund (TSF) for federal employees is a true trust fund (although it is classified for federal budget purposes as a "deposit fund"). Unlike the Social Security fund, the employee contributions to the TSF are voluntary. Those contributions, along with government matching contributions, are deposited in individual accounts for the exclusive benefit of the employees, and federal employees have elected to invest most of those deposits in Treasury securities, which are clearly "held by the public."[5]

The debt/GDP ratio is also the measure of the alleged debt burden that is best known to the press and thus to the public. The following comment by Robert Kuttner, a *Washington Post* columnist, is fairly typical:

> In fact, there is no good economic reason why the budget must achieve absolute balance, in 2002 or any other year. The real fiscal issue is whether the national debt is manageable relative to the overall economy. . . .
>
> The accumulated debt held by the public is now equal to about 55 percent of one year's economic output—a level high by recent standards but actually lower than in most industrial nations and half the level that it was right after World War II.
>
> Suppose we agree that the debt ratio should not go any higher. The long-term rate of economic growth has averaged about 2½ percent. As long as the debt grows more slowly than the economy as a whole, that debt ratio will gradually decline. That means deficits are tolerable, as long as they don't exceed 2½ percent of economic output.[6]

Really? Where is it written that it is tolerable to keep running deficits forever—to have more government than the people are willing to pay for in taxes? I reviewed all 196 books cataloged by the Library of Congress since 1968 under the heading "Debts, Public—United States"; I must have dozed off when I went by that one.

The key words in Mr. Kuttner's statement are "Suppose we agree," because there is no other basis to conclude that it is acceptable to grow deficits as fast as the economy grows. Yet this statement is probably a pretty fair representation of much of the conventional wisdom in Washington as to the appropriate level of the debt/GDP ratio—that, for some unknown reason, it is acceptable where it is but it should not go any higher.

Actually, I agree with the thrust of Mr. Kuttner's argument that the public debt is not an undue burden on the economy. Yet that fact does not justify further deficit spending. As discussed in chapter 10, deficit spending would not be justifiable even if the public debt were zero.

Figure 1-1 shows how the debt/GDP ratio has changed since it peaked at the end of World War II. The net debt in 1946 of $242 billion (the gross debt of $271 billion less the $29 billion held by government accounts) was 114 percent of GDP. The ratio declined steadily to a low of 25 percent in 1974 and then rose to approximately 50 percent in the 1992–1995 period. Thus, by this particular measure, the debt "burden" has doubled in the last 20 years, but it is less than half what it was at the end of World War II.

Where do we go from here with the debt/GDP ratio? Nobody knows. While the ratio seems to have leveled off in the last few years, as the figure indicates, the history of the ratio does not suggest any normal level or clear trend. We can project GDP, based on reasonable economic assumptions; but the debt is a political phenomenon, not an economic one, and is no more predictable than the political makeup of the U.S. Congress. (The political projection in President Clinton's 1997 budget shows the debt/GDP ratio declining gradually to 42 percent in the year 2002.)

What should the debt/GDP ratio be? Nobody knows that either. While many people might say that our long-run goal should be to eliminate the debt entirely, those who propose tax reductions or increased spending for their favorite government programs would apparently be comfortable with a higher debt/GDP ratio. Others, like

Figure 1-1 Federal debt held by the public as a percent of GDP, fiscal years 1946–1995

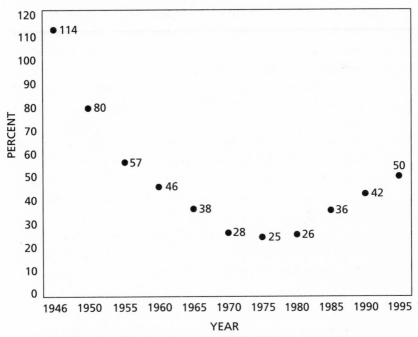

Source: Office of Management and Budget, *Analytical Perspectives, Budget of the United States Government, Fiscal Year 1997* (Washington, D.C.: GPO, 1996), 187.

Mr. Kuttner, seem to feel that it should not be any higher than it is now, but their analysis stops there.

In the absence of any consensus, or even a clear minority view, on the appropriate level of the debt/GDP ratio, one may ask whether the ratio is really important. That will be discussed in chapter 2.

DEFICIT/GDP RATIO

Another common measure of the government debt burden is the ratio of the budget deficit to the gross domestic product. Mr. Kuttner suggests that the annual deficit rate of growth should not exceed the annual rate of growth in GDP. That could be achieved on average over a period of many years, but it could not be achieved each year because the deficit increases faster when the economy slows down. Indeed, it is common to have actual *declines* in GDP in years with the greatest deficits. A weakening economy causes a decrease in incomes, and thus tax revenues, at the same time that government expenditures increase for economic assistance programs such as unemployment benefits and food stamps.

Figure 1-2 shows the deficit/GDP ratio. The postwar peak of 7.5 percent in 1946 was followed by several years of budget surpluses or relatively small deficits. The ratio stayed below 3 percent until the mid-1970s, and it has generally been in the 3 to 5 percent range during the past decade. In 1995 the ratio was 2.3 percent.

Some people worry about a rising deficit/GDP ratio because they believe that the relative increase in government borrowing has an adverse impact on the economy. The notion seems to be that the government does more harm by borrowing people's money than it does by just taking it away from them in taxes. That notion will be discussed in chapter 3.

GOVERNMENT'S SHARE OF TOTAL DEBT OUTSTANDING

The influence of the government's debt on the economy is also measured by the ratio of the net federal debt to the estimated total of public and private debt. Figure 1-3 shows a sharp decline in this federal share of total debt from 55 percent in 1950 to below 20 percent in the mid-1970s, and then a gradual increase to 26 percent in 1995.

The ratio of federal debt to total debt is a relatively obscure statistic and was in most of the 1960s and 1970s estimated by the Treasury for the sole purpose of accommodating a request from former Senator Russell B. Long of Louisiana. The Senator apparently liked to have the record show the dramatic relative decline in the federal debt in the postwar period.

As a prominent Democrat and chairman of the Senate Finance Committee, Senator Long routinely asked the Treasury to provide extensive statistical tables, which became known as the Long tables, showing the history of the federal debt relative to GDP, total debt,

Figure 1-2 Federal deficit as a percent of GDP, fiscal years 1946–1995

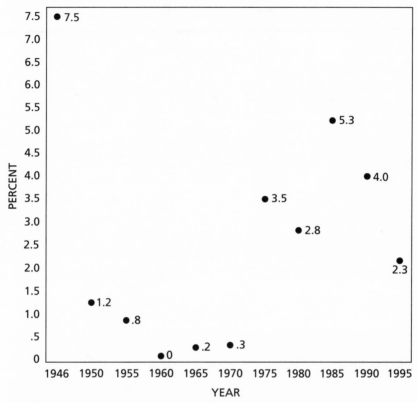

Sources: Office of Management and Budget, *Budget of the United States Government, Fiscal Year 1993, Supplement, February 1992* (Washington, D.C.: GPO, 1992), 5: 15, 16; Office of Management and Budget, *Analytical Perspectives, Budget of the United States Government, Fiscal Year 1997* (Washington, D.C.: GPO, 1996), 5: 189.

Note: During World War II the deficit/GDP ratio peaked at 31 percent in 1943. The only surplus years since the war were 1947, 1948, 1949, 1951, 1956, 1957, 1960, and 1969.

population, and prices. Apart from Senator Long, there was no other significant demand for the total debt measure, so federal agencies were generally reluctant to use their limited resources to gather the information needed to provide the estimates of private debt. Yet when the Treasury appeared before the Senate Finance Committee each year to request an increase in the statutory public debt limit, we were

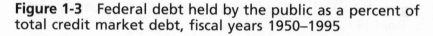

Figure 1-3 Federal debt held by the public as a percent of total credit market debt, fiscal years 1950–1995

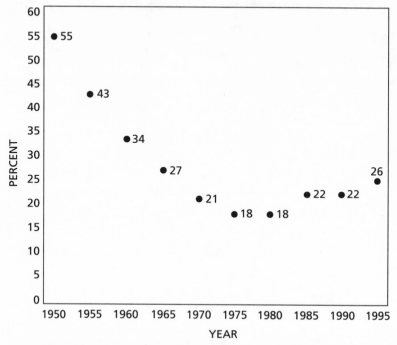

Source: Office of Management and Budget, *Analytical Perspectives, Budget of the United States Government, Fiscal Year 1997* (Washington, D.C.: GPO, 1996), 187.

advised that it would be necessary to update the Long tables before the committee would act on our request.

If Senator Long were still in the Senate, he might not be as interested in these statistics: they have been going in the other direction since the mid-1970s.

PER CAPITA DEBT

What's my share of the national debt? People are interested in that figure, which happens to be about $19,000 for each man, woman, and child in the country.[7] After deducting the government's holdings of its own debt (in the Social Security and other trust funds), the per capita debt is about $14,000. Historical trends in this statistic are meaningful only when adjusted for inflation to arrive at the real per capita debt changes. Figure 1-4 shows the steady postwar decline in the real per capita debt (in constant 1987 dollars), from more than $7,000 in 1950 to less than $4,000 in 1975, but then a sharp increase to an estimated $10,000 in 1995.

Another way to look at the individual American's liability for the national debt is to take into account the fact that the American people,

Figure 1-4   Real per capita net federal debt, fiscal years 1950–1995

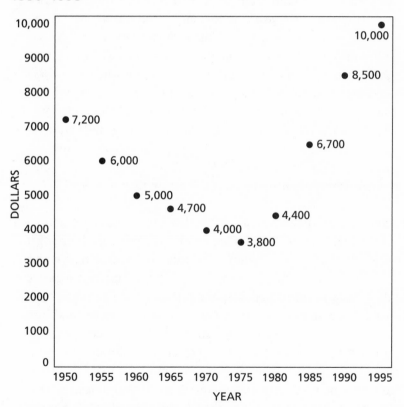

Source: Derived from debt data in Office of Management and Budget, *Analytical Perspectives, Budget of the United States Government, Fiscal Year 1996* (Washington, D.C.: GPO, 1995), 187, and population data in *Economic Report of the President, February 1995* (Washington, D.C.: GPO, 1995), 311.

collectively, own the government, its assets as well as its liabilities. More on that in chapter 2.

THE INTEREST BURDEN ON THE BUDGET

To many people, including President Clinton, perhaps the most alarming federal debt statistic is the interest on the debt. The President put it this way in his state of the union address to Congress in 1993:

> If we don't act now, you and I might not even recognize this Government 10 years from now. If we just stay with the same trends of the last 4 years, by the end of the decade the deficit will be $635 billion a year, almost 80 percent of our gross domestic product. And paying interest on that debt will be the costliest Government program of all. . . . And when Members of Congress come here, they'll be devoting over 20 cents on the dollar to interest payments, more than half of the budget to health care and to other entitlements. And you'll come here and deliberate and argue over 6 or 7 cents on the dollar, no matter what America's problems are. We will not be able to have the independence we need to chart the future that we must.[8]

The President's apparent concern is that the interest payments will be so big that there will not be enough money left in the budget to finance other spending programs. Conservatives may regard this as a blessing, while at the same time point to the interest expense as the disastrous result of deficit spending.

Figure 1-5 shows net interest payments relative to total budget outlays. After a sharp drop from more than 11 percent in 1950 to less than 8 percent in 1955, the ratio changed little over the next twenty years. Then, because of both the growth in deficit financing of government programs and increases in market rates of interest, the ratio rose sharply to more than 10 percent in 1980 and to 16 percent in 1995. The Clinton administration now expects (in the 1997 budget estimates) the ratio to decline to 12 percent by 2002. More on that in chapter 4.

Figure 1-5 Net interest on debt held by the public as a percent of total budget outlays, fiscal years 1950–1995

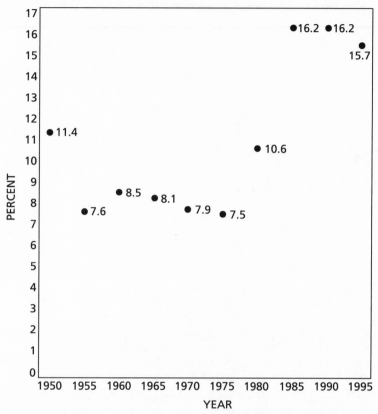

Source: Office of Management and Budget, *Analytical Perspectives, Budget of the United States Government, Fiscal Year 1997* (Washington, D.C.: GPO, 1996), 187.

THE INTEREST BURDEN ON THE ECONOMY

Similarly, as indicated in figure 1-6, the public debt interest burden on the economy, as measured by the ratio of net interest payments to GDP, increased from 1.7 percent in 1975 to 3.7 percent in 1985, but has since declined somewhat and is estimated (in the 1997 budget) to decline to 2.3 percent in 2002.

Now that we have looked at pictures of six common measures of the federal deficit/debt burden on our economy, what do we know?

Figure 1-6   Net interest on debt held by the public as a
percent of GDP, fiscal years 1950–1995

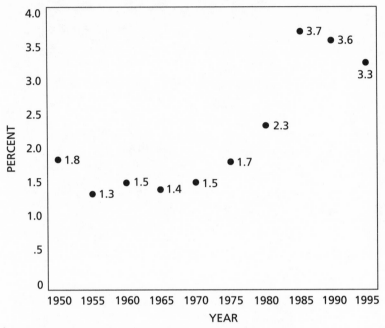

Source: Office of Management and Budget, *Analytical Perspectives, Budget of the United States
Government, Fiscal Year 1997* (Washington, D.C.: GPO, 1996), 187.

Not much. The charts do not tell us what these measures will be or
should be. Other economic statistics, such as the growth of productivity or GDP, help us to keep track of our real economic progress; and
equity measures, such as income distribution or taxes as a percentage
of our incomes, are essential to our understanding of fairness and
the role of government in our society. But the deficit/debt statistics
provide little guidance as to how well we are doing or what our
policies or goals should be. What then should we be watching? That
is what we will explore in the following chapters.

2 Myth Number One: The Debt Burden on Future Generations

L ET US NOW CONSIDER THE GREATEST, and hoariest, myth about the national debt, namely, that it is a burden on future generations of Americans.

My first insights into the depth of feeling of American business executives about the burden of the public debt were from my meetings with them in the 1960s in support of the U.S. Savings Bonds Program. At that time the Savings Bonds Division staff of the Treasury made promotional presentations to groups of local business leaders throughout the country to encourage them to support payroll savings plans for their employees. As an economist on the Treasury's debt management staff, I was occasionally asked to participate in these presentations to explain how important savings bonds are to overall public debt management.

Although the business community generally welcomed the opportunity to support savings bonds sales to raise funds that the Treasury would otherwise have to borrow in the securities markets at higher interest costs, they were deeply troubled by the growing national debt and in full accord with the statements of our political leaders that we were mortgaging our future, our children's future, our grandchildren's future—saddling unborn babies with a staggering debt burden.

A NEWBORN BABY CRIES TWICE

A representative from the Savings Bonds Division, before introducing me as the luncheon speaker, would sometimes break the ice and set the mood with the quip, "A newborn baby in this country cries twice, once on entering the world and once on realizing the size of his share of the public debt" ($19,000 in 1995). Everyone would have a good chuckle and nod knowingly at this reminder of the burden of the public debt on future generations.

This little quip may have reinforced the preconceptions of patriotic business leaders and sold some savings bonds, but it was at best a half-truth. We cannot reasonably say that today's crop of babies will "inherit" a public debt liability without noting that they will also inherit a public debt asset. Treasury debt issues, like all other debt instruments, must be liabilities of the issuer and assets of the holders of the instruments. The American people generally own the Treasury securities that make up the public debt—either directly through their holdings of savings bonds or other Treasury securities or indirectly through their banks, insurance companies, pension funds, or other institutions that invest in Treasury securities.[1] So, as any business executive should know, a liability that is offset by an asset of equal value should not be viewed as a burden.

People alive today, or at any time in the future, may properly say that the public debt is an obligation that "we owe to ourselves." They certainly cannot owe it to people who are deceased or unborn.

It is true that older people are more likely to have more savings than younger people and thus more invested in Treasury securities; but that should not be viewed as a burden on the young. Indeed, young people borrowing to buy their first home benefit from the fact that the savings of older people add to the flow of funds needed to finance mortgages. Yet in 1993 the twentysomething group Lead . . . or Leave expressed its concern about the legacy of the national debt by picketing the Washington office of the American Association of Retired Persons.

People in their twenties may have a legitimate complaint that their elders have not saved *enough*. We expect each generation to add to the pool of capital that it inherits. That's progress. It is not enough just to maintain the value of our inheritance. Economists generally agree that the personal savings rate in this country has been too low in recent years and that people have not been saving enough for retirement. Put another way, people have been spending too much of their income on current consumption and not enough on investment in the future, be that investment in Treasury securities or any other form of investment.

So what is the basis for the concern about the burden of the public debt on future generations? Is it that old people might reduce their investment in the future by selling their Treasury securities and going on a luxury spending binge (as suggested by the popular bumper sticker, "We're Spending Our Children's Inheritance")? Not likely. The investments in Treasury, or other, securities for the benefit of older people are largely held in trust funds, such as Social Security or the nearly 1 million other public and private pension and retirement funds in this country, or in life insurance, health insurance, or other funds for the payment of death, medical, or accidental benefits.

Only 9 percent of publicly held Treasury securities are held directly by individuals, largely in the form of long-term investments in tax-deferred U.S. savings bonds, and a good portion of those savings will probably be passed on to beneficiaries or used to cover medical expenses of the elderly that might otherwise be financed by taxpayers through Medicaid (see chapter 5).

Ultimately, of course, the assets represented by the volume of Treasury securities outstanding (which will probably continue to grow each year, as it has since 1969) will be passed on to each new generation. Old people die, and they can't take it with them. Yet the myth persists that by passing on the national debt we are borrowing from the future.

Real borrowing from the future, as indicated above, occurs when our "excess consumption" today eats into the production of future Americans. Some might say, "How can that be? Surely we cannot consume what has not yet been produced." The answer, of course, is that future production depends on the level of today's investment. Government spending on roads, bridges, sewers, and other public facilities represents an investment for the benefit of future Americans, which could increase their productivity and standard of living. By contrast, government spending for many operating subsidy programs for farming and other businesses may stimulate current consumption at the expense of investment. Similarly, spending for welfare programs for the poor or infirm, or others with a high propensity to consume, however worthwhile, may be viewed as current consumption rather than as investment in the future.

Future production will also be affected by today's tax policies. Federal tax incentives that encourage savings, such as individual retirement accounts or tax-deferred savings plans, increase the funds available for investment in the future. On the other hand, increasing the tax on investment income and using the revenue for government subsidy payments to tobacco growers would be a double negative for the future.

So we cannot generalize about the future impact of government spending or taxation. It depends on how the particular tax or expenditure affects consumption or investment.[2]

WHY GOVERNMENT FINANCES AREN'T LIKE FAMILY FINANCES

In his January 1981 inaugural address, Ronald Reagan said, "You and I, as individuals, can, by borrowing, live beyond our means, but only for a limited period of time. Why then do we think collectively, as a nation, we are not bound by that same limitation? For decades we have piled deficit upon deficit, mortgaging our future and our children's future for the temporary convenience of the present. To continue this long trend is to guarantee tremendous social, cultural, political and economic upheavals."

President Reagan's predecessors had left him a national debt of approximately $1 trillion. Eight years later, after Mr. Reagan left office, the debt had grown to approximately $3 trillion.[3] Fortunately, however, his dire predictions did not come true. The United States is still the strongest and freest economy in the world—indeed the only remaining superpower—and some would argue that President Reagan's borrowing to support his commitment to maintaining a strong military had a lot to do with our winning the Cold War.

The answer to President Reagan's question is that collectively, as a nation, we are in fact not bound by the same limitations on individual borrowers because, unlike individual borrowers, we owe the debt to ourselves.

Much of the confusion over the burden of the public debt arises from the understandable tendency to try to model government financing after the financing of an individual family or business. Politicians often add to this confusion. A familiar scene might be a politician making a campaign speech at a town meeting in a rural district and saying, "Henry, can you run a deficit in your farm business every year and just make up the difference by borrowing?" Henry, of course, responds with a lusty "Hell, no!" Then the politician says, "You're darn right, and neither can Washington, but that is what Washington has been doing, and this country is headed for bankruptcy. Elect me to Congress and I'll go to Washington and fight to change that."

Well, perhaps that's what Henry wanted to hear, in which case the politician practiced good political followership. Political leadership might have gone something like this:

"Henry, if your daughter borrows money from you does that increase your family's debt?

"No. It's all in the family."

"If you borrow from other people in your town does that increase the debt of the townspeople?

"Well, I guess not. It's all in the town."

"That's right, Henry, and that's the way it is with the national debt. It's all in the U.S., except for the portion held by foreigners. We the people both owe the debt and own the debt. The U.S. is us."

As one of my favorite economists, Herbert Stein, put it, "The government is no one. There is nobody here but us people."[4]

HOW PAST PRESIDENTS VIEWED THE NATIONAL DEBT

It may be that the phobia about the national debt burden is so deeply ingrained because of the doomsaying by our leaders over the past two hundred years. Virtually from the birth of this nation, American presidents have recorded their deep concerns about the seeming irresponsibility of burdening future generations with a national debt.

In our first president's farewell address, George Washington said that the government's debt should be paid off to avoid "ungenerously throwing upon posterity the burdens which we ourselves ought to bear."

Consider also the following excerpt from a book by Peter Peterson, a prominent investment banker and former secretary of Commerce, in which he expresses great concern that the national debt will be an unbearable burden on his grandchildren:

> More than two centuries ago, Thomas Jefferson wrote a letter to James Madison in which he warned of the utter inappropriateness in a democracy of a value system that allows the debts of one generation to burden the next. The earth, he wrote, should by all rights belong to the generation alive at any given time. He observed that if one generation could leave its debts to encumber the next, "then the earth would belong to the dead and not to the living generation."
>
> Contemplating the issue of national debt, Jefferson urged nascent democracies to "declare in the constitution they are forming, that neither the legislature nor the nation itself can validly contract more debt than they can pay within their own age."[5]

Could Jefferson really have believed that the earth could possibly belong to the dead? What does that mean—that future generations will come to our graves every six months and deposit the interest payments on the public debt by our headstones?

Would Jefferson, or perhaps Peter Peterson, have suggested that the United States accept defeat after Pearl Harbor rather than rely as it did on the long-term public debt financing of World War II? (The alternative of financing a major war from current tax revenues is not workable, as discussed in chapter 3.) Are we to believe that fiscal probity, as Jefferson and Peterson define it, is more important than national survival?

Perhaps it is unfair to judge Jefferson's comments by today's standards of financial or economic analysis. But what about Peter Peterson? He must be sophisticated in the ways of both Washington and Wall Street. Yet he made the following statement: "In sum, the hard truth is that *full disclosure and honest accounting would show that today's generation of workforce entrants is the first in American history to be bankrupt.* A good indication of how bad they're doing is how well a certain firm called Crane and Company is doing. That's the firm that makes the paper on which U.S. currency and other financial instruments like Treasury bonds are printed. It has been reporting record sales."[6]

Bankrupt, according to *Webster's,* means "reduced to a state of financial ruin." In accounting terms, a bankrupt person, organization, generation, or nation has more liabilities than assets. According to U.S. government budget figures, the estimated assets of this nation as of the end of the fiscal year 1995 were $55.0 trillion, but its liabilities (net claims of foreigners on the United States) were only $.9 trillion. Thus, the budget reports a national wealth balance of $54.1 trillion, compared with $16.7 trillion in 1960, $25.7 trillion in 1970, $40.2 trillion in 1980, and $50.7 trillion in 1990. On a per capita basis, that works out to $205,100 for each man, woman, or child in 1995, compared with just $92,200 in 1960 (adjusted for inflation in 1995 dollars). So real individual wealth has more than doubled since 1960 (see table 2-1).

So how can Peter Peterson rightly say that "today's generation of workforce entrants is the first in American history to be bankrupt?" He cannot.

As to Mr. Peterson's portrayal of the fortunes of Treasury's printer, Crane and Company, U.S. currency represents less than 10 percent of the U.S. money supply, which is largely in the form of deposits in financial institutions. Also, currency is generally used for relatively small transactions and is the slowest growing component of the U.S. money supply, especially as people have shifted more and more to credit cards. The growth in currency is essentially a function of consumer tastes. The Federal Reserve banks will provide as much currency as people want (which is not true of the total money supply). Currency certainly has nothing to do with the health of our economy or the financial future of our children. (There has been increased demand for U.S. currency by foreigners; but that is a very positive development,

Table 2-1   National wealth (end of fiscal year, trillions of dollars)

	1960	1970	1980	1990	1995
Total assets	16.5	25.5	39.7	51.0	55.0
Publicly owned physical assets[a]	2.7	3.5	5.2	5.0	4.9
Privately owned physical assets	7.3	10.5	18.1	20.9	20.7
Education capital	6.1	10.8	15.4	23.5	27.5
R&D capital	0.3	0.7	1.0	1.6	1.9
Less: Net claims of foreigners on					
U.S.	−0.2	−0.2	−0.5	0.3	0.9
Equals: Balance	16.7	25.7	40.2	50.7	54.1
Per capita (thousands of 1995					
dollars)	92.2	125.5	176.1	202.1	205.1

Source: Office of Management and Budget, *Analytical Perspectives, Budget of the United States Government, Fiscal Year 1997* (Washington, D.C.: GPO, 1996), 27.

Notes: Physical assets include factories, machinery, office buildings, residential structures, land, automobiles, consumer appliances, and government's physical assets, such as military hardware and highways. *Education capital* is an estimate of the nation's investment in human capital. As stated by the Office of Management and Budget, "The idea is to measure how much it would cost to reeducate the U.S. workforce at today's prices."

[a]Includes federal and state and local governments.

since foreign holdings of our currency represent interest-free loans to the United States.)

Moreover, the Treasury stopped the printing of Treasury bonds and other marketable debt securities in 1986 (many years before the publication of Mr. Peterson's book). All such securities are now issued in book-entry form, and printed securities have long been regarded as a needless expense and an invitation to theft and counterfeiting. Wall street professionals should be keenly aware of this.

As a former secretary of Commerce and prominent Wall Street banker, Mr. Peterson was in an enviable position to perform a great public service of enlightening the American people about their national debt. He did not do that. Instead, he perpetuated the old myths and thus compounded the public confusion, cynicism, and loss of confidence in government. This failure of leadership, not just by Mr. Peterson but by nearly all of our current and former leaders, is dismaying. A great irony, though, is the fact that politicians have been so successful in scaring people about the alleged national debt crisis that people are now throwing them out of office for not resolving it. Voters may forever be fooled by the economics of the national debt, but they do recognize hypocrisy. (I find this an interesting facet of Abraham Lincoln's ". . . you can't fool all of the people all of the time.")

Moving on to the twentieth century, we find the following presidential beatitude: " 'Blessed are the young, for they shall inherit the national debt,' quipped Herbert Hoover."[7] More recently, in his January 1960 state of the union message, President Eisenhower said: "Personally, I do not feel that any amount can be properly called a surplus as long as the nation is in debt. I prefer to think of such an item as a reduction on our children's inherited mortgage."[8]

I was a Treasury Department economist at the time Eisenhower made that statement about the then annual federal budget surplus and the as yet unpaid World War II debt. Nearly all economists rejected Eisenhower's view that the public debt would be a burden on future generations,[9] although I do not recall any criticism of the Eisenhower statement from politicians. Indeed, the political debate was over how soon the debt must be paid off rather than whether it should be paid off.

So there was little apparent difference between presidential attitudes toward the Revolutionary War debt and the World War II debt. Notably, Abraham Lincoln had a different view of the Civil War debt. He may have been the only president to recognize both sides of the ledger—that for every borrower there must be a lender. James Savage, author of *Balanced Budgets and American Politics,* writes: "In his 1864 Annual Message to Congress, Lincoln remarked, 'The great advantage of citizens being creditors as well as debtors, with relation to the public debt, is obvious. Men can readily perceive that they cannot be much oppressed by a debt which they owe to themselves.' "[10]

Lincoln was reportedly motivated to make that statement to calm public fears about the growing Civil War debt. But at least for one brief shining moment in the history of our national debt, good economics happened to coincide with good politics. But look now at the words of a leading spokesman of the party of Lincoln, Newt Gingrich: "For the children trapped in poverty, for the children whose futures are trapped by a government debt they're going to have to pay, we have an obligation tonight to talk about the legacy we're leaving our children and grandchildren."[11] At least as far as the national debt is concerned, Mr. Gingrich's Contract with America appears to be nothing more than new voices spouting old myths.

WHO PAID FOR WORLD WAR II?

By the reckoning of Washington, Jefferson, Eisenhower, Reagan, Clinton—perhaps all presidents except Lincoln—and many other notables such as Ross Perot, Peter Peterson, and Newt Gingrich, we apparently have never paid for World War II.

The federal debt at the end of the war was approximately $270 billion, which was about equal to total defense spending in the four fiscal years 1942–1945. World War II was financed largely by debt (deficit spending) rather than by taxes. The debt was commonly viewed by politicians as a staggering legacy of the war. So it should not be surprising that after the war there was intense political debate about the future burden of the war debt, even though economists generally recognized that the cost of the war could not be shifted to the future.

The economic burden of World War II, in terms of debt or otherwise, was borne by the Americans who made the sacrifices at the time: no new cars from 1942 through 1945, a ration of a few gallons of gas a week for pleasure driving, and scarcities of housing and consumer goods across the board. Americans could not consume the tanks and guns they produced in the war effort. Instead, they increased their savings, which became a source of funds for the government's war debt. In addition to the stepped-up sales of Treasury marketable securities, the government conducted massive campaigns of patriotic appeals to small savers to help finance the war effort by buying U.S. savings bonds (then called war bonds and defense bonds).[12] The war was thus paid for at the time, and future generations were benefited, not burdened, by the national security then achieved.

The greatest cost of World War II, of course, was borne by those who paid the ultimate price . . . and by the loved ones left behind. I was just a boy at the time, but I will never forget the shock that went through my neighborhood in Somerville, Massachusetts, at each report of the loss of a neighborhood serviceman in the early days of the war in the Pacific.

When a serviceman was killed in World War II, the government presented a gold star to his mother, which was often displayed in the front window of the home. It seemed the war had barely started when gold stars began appearing throughout the neighborhood. There were so many on one nearby street that the street was renamed Gold Star Road. The mothers of those young men and hundreds of thousands of other "Gold Star Mothers" knew who paid the cost of World War II. The cost was theirs, and the benefit (national security) is ours.

We never paid off the war debt—$270 billion plus interest—and today's federal debt is roughly equal to it. At an annual interest rate of 6 percent (the Treasury's approximate average annual borrowing cost since 1946), $270 billion would grow in fifty years to approximately $5 trillion, which happens to be only slightly less than the $5.2 trillion estimated federal debt at the end of fiscal year 1996. Thus, had we paid off the debt from World War II (including interest), we might have little or no federal debt today (albeit based on the very questionable assumption of "all other things being equal").

What does that mean? That the cost, or debt burden, of World War II has been shifted to this generation? Or that, if we go another fifty years without paying off the debt (with accrued interest continuing at 6 percent), we will shift the World War II debt burden—then $96 trillion—to our grandchildren in the year 2046, one hundred years after the end of the war? No. Whatever the size of the federal debt in 2046, the people alive at that time will not owe it to us or to the World War II generation. They will owe it to one another. They will inherit both the Treasury security assets and the public debt payment liabilities.

Had we borrowed from other countries to help finance World War II (which we did not), and had that borrowing resulted in a net foreign investment in the United States at the end of the war, then there would have been a shifting of costs to post–World War II Americans. Yet that would have been an international shift, not an intergenerational shift. Moreover, proper cost-benefit analysis surely would have shown that the war costs were nominal compared with the benefits of victory to future generations of Americans. What price freedom?

Perhaps most people would agree (I would) that debt financing is justifiable to fight a war to repel aggression; that the first law of nature, and of nations, is self-preservation; and that if the only means to that end is to beg, borrow, or steal, so be it. Indeed, we have an obligation to future generations, in the words of our Constitution, to "provide for the common defence . . . and secure the Blessings of Liberty to ourselves and our Posterity."

Some might argue, perhaps with less moral authority, that deficit financing of a defense buildup to prevent war, such as in the 1980s, is also justifiable. Absent a clear and present danger to our national security, however, defense spending should in my view be subject to the discipline of a balanced budget requirement.

ACCOUNTING FOR THE COSTS OF PUBLIC WORKS PROJECTS

Some others have argued further that borrowing is an appropriate means of financing the government's capital expenditures. There have been many proposals over the years for a "business-type" capital budget, which would permit borrowing for government expenditures on the construction of buildings or other public works projects or vehicles or equipment with a useful life of more than one year.

Today, when the federal government purchases land, buildings, or other capital items, it counts such purchases as current expenditures and thus treats them in the federal budget in the same way as operating expenses for, say, government workers' salaries, travel expenses, or paper and pencils. Consequently, to minimize apparent budget costs in the short run, the government has often chosen to rent or lease privately owned buildings, even though government ownership of the buildings would have been much less costly to taxpayers. Private corporations, by contrast, generally separate current operating expenditures from capital expenditures and view borrowing as appropriate for the latter. Thus the costs of a building are spread over many years, which is important to the determination of business profits and taxes. Also, private individuals who otherwise avoid debt generally view borrowing as appropriate to finance the purchase of a capital item such as a house or, for many, a car.

This difference in accounting between government and private business produces some anomalous measures of saving and investment in our economy. If the government constructs a new building, the construction cost adds to the government's budget deficit and is thus counted as dissaving in our national accounting statements. Yet when a private business constructs a new building the accounting is just the opposite—the building is counted as investment. Accordingly, if the government decides to lease the building, to avoid the political problems from including the up-front construction cost in the current budget deficit, the construction cost counts as private investment, even though the sole purpose of the building is to house a government facility.

Some proponents of a capital budget for the federal government see it as a way to increase spending for public facility programs. Expenditures for capital items would be treated as investments and would no longer be included in current operating expenses or in the current operating deficit at the time of the spending. Such expenditures would result in annual depreciation expenses that would show up later in the budgets of future presidents, but the current president would get the political credit for the projects. That accounting change, however, would not necessarily reduce current budget deficits, since budget expenditures, say, in 1996 and thereafter, would presumably be increased by the amount of depreciation charges for buildings and other capital items acquired by the government prior to 1996.[13]

Others say that a capital budget would instill discipline in the process of federal borrowing; borrowing might generally be permitted only for facilities that provide long-term benefits. Opponents counter that there is a greater need for discipline in spending, not borrowing, and that capital spending should be subject to the discipline of tax financing.

A detailed discussion of the above capital budget issues appears in the President's budget for fiscal year 1996.[14]

Some argue that a capital budget would ensure greater intergenerational equity, since the principal and interest payments on the borrowing would come out of the taxes paid by future users of the facilities financed by the borrowing. That argument is wrong. A change in government bookkeeping or method of financing would not change the economic or intergenerational effects of government expenditures.

Consider the simple proposition of, say, $100 billion of new Treasury borrowing to finance investment in the construction of new bridges, sewers, roads, or other public works projects. Obviously, the generation that provides the labor and other economic resources to build these long-term projects, as well as the savings to buy the securities, is the generation that bears the cost. Succeeding generations benefit from this inheritance of new public facilities; they also inherit $100 billion in financial assets (the Treasury securities originally issued to investors now deceased), which are offset by their liabilities, as taxpayers, to service or repay the debt.

Had the $100 billion in public facilities been financed with new taxes, instead of debt, that fact in itself would not have affected the intergenerational equity outcome—succeeding generations would still have a net increase of $100 billion in physical assets and no increase in the net of their financial assets and financial liabilities.

The burden of government spending on the *current* generation of taxpayers may well be quite different if the spending is financed by borrowing rather than by taxation, but that is an *intragenerational* effect. (See in chapter 5 the discussion of a Treasury study of the burden of taxation and borrowing.)

So it is wrong to say that the cost burden is shifted to succeeding generations simply because the means of financing is debt instead of taxes. This fact was recognized in part in the budget submitted by the President to Congress in February 1995:

But the deficit has another side. If the Government borrows money to finance investments that truly will pay for themselves in the future, then future generations who inherit the debt also reap the benefits of the investments. If, for instance, the Government borrows money to build new roads and bridges needed

to make the economy more productive, then living standards
will rise and future generations will have the higher incomes
they need to pay off the debt and still live better than they would
have otherwise.[15]

That statement is correct as far as it goes, but it should have gone
on to recognize that future generations do not need higher incomes
to pay off the debt. As indicated above, those generations will inherit
the assets as well as the liabilities represented by the federal debt. So
if they pay off the debt, they will pay it to themselves.

Nevertheless, let us consider the apparent suggestion in the budget
that it is acceptable to have a deficit equal to the amount of spending
for productive investments. What then is the factual situation? How
much of the $164 billion deficit for the fiscal year 1995 may be
attributed to government investment spending? The administration's
answer is suggested in another part of the budget documents: "The
Federal Government is, by far, the Nation's single largest investor.
In 1995, it will spend an estimated $235 billion [the actual figure was
$237 billion] for physical investment, such as structures, roads, and
equipment, and 'intangible' investments, such as education and training and research and development (R&D)—about 10 percent of total
investment in the U.S. economy." After some discussion of the long-
term public benefits of these investments, the statement concludes,
"In sum, this budget provides for investment in the truest sense of
the word—only in areas that the private sector could not or would
not develop."[16]

What does this mean—that it would have been acceptable to
borrow another $73 billion (237 − 164) in 1995 (and reduce taxes
by a like amount) since the money would be used for productive
investments for the future? No, that would not have been acceptable.
Proper capital budgeting would require that the $237 billion figure
be reduced by a substantial (but unknown) amount to cover the
depreciation charges against the government's investments in prior
years.[17] Is it worthwhile trying to figure out what that depreciation
would be? No. In fact, it's irrelevant. The whole concept of government
borrowing for "investment" expenditures is impractical. It would lead

to endless debate over the definition of investment, as special interest groups rushed to demonstrate that their favorite programs yield future benefits and should thus be counted as investment and largely excluded from the current budget deficit and the constraints on current spending.

For example, the $237 billion investment figure includes just $98 billion in the Defense Department area for research and development, education and training, and other investments for the future (see table 2-2). By this reckoning the rest of the $266 billion Defense budget, which is largely for Defense Department personnel ($72 billion) and operation and maintenance ($94 billion) expenses, does not meet the test of investment for the future. Is our future national

Table 2-2 Federal investment outlays, fiscal year 1995 (billions of dollars)

Major physical capital investment	
Direct	
National defense	59.9
Nondefense	19.5
Total direct	79.3
Grants to state and local governments	39.6
Total major physical	118.9
Conduct of research and development	
National defense	37.7
Nondefense	30.7
Total R&D	68.4
Conduct of education and training	
Grants to state and local governments	24.7
Direct	21.2
Total education and training	45.9
Total major investment	233.2
Miscellaneous physical investment	
Commodity inventories	−0.9
Other direct investment	4.5
Total miscellaneous	3.6
Total investment	236.8

Source: Office of Management and Budget, *Analytical Perspectives, Budget of the United States Government, Fiscal Year 1997* (Washington, D.C.: GPO, 1996), 93.

security really better protected by research and development than it is by a ready force? The entire Defense Department budget, if it makes sense at all in a time of peace, is for preparedness, which must be viewed as investment for the future.

On the other hand, consider a situation in which, say, $100 million is borrowed by the government for the construction of a virtually useless public facility, say, an elaborate and unneeded federal office building in the rural district of a representative who chairs a House appropriations subcommittee. This monumental white elephant is duly named after the chair of the subcommittee and is thus preserved as a permanent drain of federal taxpayer funds. If we were to raise taxes by an additional $100 million to retire this portion of the public debt, the white elephant (and the drain) would still remain. The building is not investment in the future; it is disinvestment. The economic damage was done when this "pork barrel" project was built, and it cannot be undone by some financial legerdemain. Why perpetuate the farce by pretending that the building is economically viable and capable of producing revenue to repay the indebtedness incurred to finance its construction?

There are great differences between a governmental entity and a profit-oriented, taxpaying, competitive business. The business of government is government, not "business." The many private purposes of capital budgeting, including the determination of current business costs, prices, and profits, are largely irrelevant to the federal government.

Moreover, government cannot confine its scope to its own set of books, to its own receipts, expenditures, assets, and liabilities. A federal grant to a local government to finance a public building or other capital facility is just as much a capital investment by the federal government as if it were constructed by the federal government itself. The government must look at the impacts of its actions on the broader society, what economists call "externalities," which cannot be easily reduced to bookkeeping entries. For example, federal spending to finance programs to reduce teenage smoking might well be more than repaid by reductions in the future costs of health care.

FUTURE BENEFITS FROM CURRENT CONSUMPTION

While future generations may be net beneficiaries of current government spending for national defense or for the construction of public facilities or other capital expenditures, what good will come to them from today's government spending for benefit payments for current consumption under social and other programs? The advocates of these programs undoubtedly would say they are highly beneficial, if not essential, to our future. Government spending on education, health, the environment, and certain other social programs might well be viewed as appropriate investments in our children's future that fully justify any borrowing necessary to finance them.

Indeed, borrowing to pay teachers' salaries or to pay for the counseling of troubled teenagers is a greater investment in our future than borrowing to construct an unneeded highway or a pile of bricks and mortar built as a testimony to Senator Blowhard. Surely, such pork barrel public works spending should be subject to fiscal restraints at least as rigorous as those imposed on education and training.

With or without a capital budget, there is no clear answer to the question of which categories of government spending should be financed by borrowing and which should be financed by taxes. That is no problem, because the question is not important. The important questions have to do with the spending itself. Is it essential? Is it good for the country, for now and for the future? Should it be done by government or by the private sector? Are we spending too little on investments in the future and too much on current consumption? The way to ensure proper consideration of these questions is to subject all spending to the discipline of a balanced budget requirement. Deficit financing is justified only for war or unexpected events.

When I was a boy I was struck by a sign in the window of a donut shop in Boston. It read, "As you wander on through life, brother, whatever be your goal, keep your eye upon the donut and not upon the hole." The donut is government spending. The hole is the deficit.

One congressman made the point quite forcibly in the course of congressional debate on the floor of the House of Representatives prior to the enactment of the Omnibus Budget Reconciliation Act of 1993. He held up a large sign that read, "IT'S SPENDING, STUPID!"

CONCLUSION

The national debt is not a burden on future generations because, as a group, each will owe the debt to itself, not to the deceased or the unborn. The burden on future generations from government actions today is determined by the nature of government spending, not whether that spending is financed from taxation or debt. While some government spending is wasteful, future generations will benefit from prudent government spending for national security, health, education, roads, bridges, and other public facility investments in the future.

To understand the impact of government actions on future generations, we must look primarily to the real economy, not the way the government is financed. Our focus should be on the utilization of human and material resources, not financial resources. As each generation inherits the wealth of this nation—a body of knowledge as well as physical resources—it should add to that wealth and leave more behind for the next generation. That's progress. That's what we owe our grandchildren.

3 Myth Number Two: Crowding Out

THE SECOND MOST POPULAR MYTH about government budget deficits is that they "crowd out" private investments. It is commonly accepted among political leaders that Treasury borrowing to finance a deficit adds to total credit demands in financial markets and puts upward pressure on interest rates. Marginal borrowers who are unwilling or unable to pay the higher interest rates are thus said to be crowded out of the credit market.

In fact, as mentioned in chapter 1, Treasury deficits actually tend to be biggest when the economy is weak, as tax revenues decline and government spending increases, for example, for unemployment benefits and food stamps. At such times private credit demands and interest rates tend to decrease, not increase.

Yet the "crowding out" view is supported by many economists, including some who believe that government deficits are not a problem at times when private savings are adequate to meet the economy's investment needs. In the words of one such economist, "Deficits are a problem because they absorb savings that would otherwise be available to finance investment. If we had saved more even the outsized Reagan deficits need not have posed a problem. In Japan, for example, the central government's deficit during the last decade has averaged 6 percent of total income versus 3 percent in America."[1] That economist, Benjamin Friedman, is referring to the widely recognized fact that the very high private savings rates in Japan helped the Japanese to achieve great economic successes in the 1980s, in spite of a decade of enormous government deficits, which were twice the size of ours relative to the size of the respective economies.

NEITHER A BORROWER NOR A SPENDER BE

Political leaders seem given to less qualified statements of the crowding-out problem. President Clinton stated: "That's why we've got to reduce the debt, because it is crowding out other activities that we ought to be engaged in and that the American people ought to be engaged in."[2] If the President meant that the government spending from the borrowed funds was less worthy than some other private or public spending he had in mind, then the remedy is simply to eliminate the less worthy spending. That remedy would also apply if the less worthy spending were financed from tax revenues (rather than from borrowing).

Implicit in the crowding-out argument is the notion that private spending or investment is frustrated more by government borrowing than by government taxation. That notion just does not pass the test of common sense. When people ponder whether they can afford a particular expenditure or investment, they presumably consider their net financial position. Government borrowing does not reduce the net worth of the private sector—taxation does. Surely, taxation is at least as confiscatory as borrowing. (As discussed in chapter 2, the impact of taxation on investment depends on the type of tax and the incidence, or burden, of that tax.)

As one writer put it, in commenting on the government's extraction of funds from the private economy, "Whether that extraction is through taxation or borrowing makes no real economic difference. Government borrowing does reduce private funds available for investment—but those funds are just as unavailable if they have been taxed away. In fact, taxes may discourage production more."[3]

So an astute taxpayer should not be taken in by a politician who says, "I am increasing your taxes in order to reduce the deficit and thus reduce the government borrowing that crowds out your private borrowing and investment." The taxpayer's proper response might be, "Just leave my taxes alone so I can increase my private investments without your help, thank you." Perhaps the politician believes the investment decisions should not be left to ordinary people, in which case the political debate should be couched in those terms.

THE REAL FACTORS IN CROWDING OUT

It is the government spending that crowds out other activities, not the borrowing. For example, when the government builds a new federal office building, it must acquire the land, the equipment and materials, and the personnel to get the job done. There are only so many qualified architects, engineers, tradespeople, and other essential personnel available at any one time. Those are the real economic factors of production—land, labor, and capital—and the government's competition for them tends to drive up their price and reduce their availability for alternative uses in the private sector. That preemption of real resources by the government is the significant economic event that should command our attention. That is real crowding out, and it is just as real when it is financed by higher taxes as when it is financed by more government borrowing.

Some economists argue that government spending does not crowd out private spending when the economy is less than fully employed, because the government spending utilizes labor and other resources that would have been idle. The problem with that argument is that idle resources are generally the least efficient and are thus not the resources that win government contracts.

Again, this is just common sense. The abundance of nature is not without limit; at any given time and place there is a limited supply to meet current demand for real estate, skilled labor, equipment, and materials. If the government commands more of it, there is less left for private purposes. This is not true of credit. Credit does not come from nature. We create it when we borrow from our relatives, delay this month's credit card bill, or dodge our bookie.

Both the total amount and the allocation of credit are heavily influenced by government actions, not only by the monetary policies of the Federal Reserve Board but also by the many federal program agencies providing credit assistance for housing, agriculture, education, and virtually every sector of the economy (as discussed in chapter 7).

Government borrowing itself is not a significant event. What counts is what the government does with the borrowed funds. To be sure, borrowing to finance current government purchases of goods and services does have economic impacts, but the impacts are from the spending, not the borrowing.

The government does a great deal of seasonal borrowing to build up its cash balances in anticipation of certain periods during each year when spending is high or tax receipts are low. In this way the government's "checking accounts" have fluctuated from just a few billion dollars to more than $50 billion within a year. Such seasonal borrowing should have no economic impact because the government does not do anything with the money. It leaves it in the banking system for others to use.

Also, government borrowing to finance government lending may have only marginal effects on the economy or on the total supply of credit. The government is a major lender, with greater than $163 billion in direct loans outstanding for assistance to virtually every sector of our domestic economy and for foreign assistance as well.[4]

FROM *DISINTERMEDIATION* TO *SECURITIZATION*

In the 1960s and 1970s, there was some merit to the argument that Treasury borrowing crowded out private borrowing and thus private investment. Back then financial markets were much more compartmentalized.

For example, housing credit was typically provided by savings and loan associations from funds obtained at relatively modest rates of interest from individual depositors. The government did not permit the associations to raise interest rates on deposits beyond specified levels. During periods of business expansion, when market interest rates were increasing, depositors would withdraw funds from the associations and invest in Treasury or other marketable securities at higher interest rates. In that way the associations were forced to reduce their lending, and housing investment was thus said to be crowded out by government borrowing.

That process, by which the flow of funds through financial intermediaries, such as savings and loan associations, was interrupted
during periods of rising market rates of interest, was called *disintermediation*. But this had nothing to do with the federal deficit—
disintermediation occurred even during years when the government
ran a budget surplus. So long as there was a federal debt, disintermediation into Treasury securities would occur. In fact, a relatively small
portion of new security issues by the Treasury has been for financing
the deficit. Currently, more than 90 percent of Treasury's new issues
of bills, notes, and bonds in a typical quarter is to refinance maturing
securities (see table 4-1 in chapter 4).

Even if there had been no Treasury debt, the wave of disintermediation would not have been held back—it would have broken through
at some other channel, perhaps into federal agency, corporate, or
municipal securities.

But the disintermediation problem was largely resolved in the
early 1980s when the government phased out the caps on interest
rates paid by banks and savings institutions and when mortgage
lenders generally had found alternative sources of funds. They now
have financing techniques that enable them to sell their mortgage
loans in the securities markets and use the sales proceeds to make new
loans. (One well-known technique is the mortgage-backed security
guaranteed by the Government National Mortgage Association.)

Similarly, the financing of loans to individual consumers and to
businesses from bank deposits has been displaced to a large extent
by credit cards, commercial paper, and other securities market credit.

So disintermediation is now ancient history. The word has virtually dropped out of our financial lexicon. Good riddance. It was one
of the most hated words of its time, especially by financial journalists
who had to cope with such a mouthful in their day-to-day reporting.
Ironically, the new securities market financing techniques have been
dubbed *securitization*—not much of a linguistic improvement.

A QUESTION OF PRICE

While that securitization of credit markets in the 1970s and 1980s
has substantially reduced institutional impediments to the *availability*

of credit, I am not suggesting that borrowers are not crowded out by increases in the *price* of credit. Clearly, many would-be home buyers drop out of the market when interest rates on home mortgages rise to levels they are unable or unwilling to pay. Similarly, many prospective business ventures are undoubtedly abandoned or delayed as their projected profitability is diminished by increased financing costs.

Yet we should not accept the argument that rising interest rates are caused by government deficits. Economists and market experts generally agree that short-term interest rates are determined largely by the monetary policies of the Federal Reserve Board (commonly known as "the Fed") and that the Fed is concerned primarily with fighting inflation in the prices of goods and services in our economy. Thus the Fed leans toward higher interest rates, which of course increase the price of money relative to the price of goods and services.

It should be noted that the Fed must operate under the severe constraints of imperfect and untimely information. Also, the Fed is a creature of Congress and must be sensitive to the political winds from Capitol Hill, which can blow the "independent" Fed off course with hurricane speed. The Fed is well aware of its limitations. One of the favorite sayings (at least within my earshot) of Arthur Burns, that distinguished economist and former chairman of the Federal Reserve Board, was, "It's a big country out there. We don't really know what's going on."

We often hear that the Fed views government deficits as inflationary and will respond to deficit financing by putting upward pressure on interest rates. Yet, if the Fed is doing its job, it should be responding to the real inflation threat, which is government spending, not borrowing. Also, as discussed below, economic studies have found no significant relationship between government deficits and interest rates. Long-term interest rates as well are heavily influenced by inflation expectations, since the market value of long-term bonds falls as commodity prices and interest rates rise.

Inflation itself is generally caused by increased economic activity as the growing demand for goods and services leads to price pressures throughout the economy. Such economic expansion is generally accompanied by expansion in the supply of money and credit (to the extent permitted by the Fed) for business investment, housing, and other private purposes. Yet the government's borrowing to finance budget deficits tends to contract at such times, in part because of the increased tax revenues and decreased spending (for unemployment and other benefits for the needy) that accompany an expanding economy.

Why then are politicians so seemingly bereft of common sense on the crowding-out question? Surely there is nothing in recent economic history to support their mistaken notions. For example, during the period of greatest growth in the federal debt, from $1 trillion in 1981 to $4 trillion in 1992, interest rates on three-year Treasury securities actually *declined*, from 14 percent to 5 percent. Some economists would argue with that example, saying that such nominal rates of interest should be adjusted for inflation expectations. For example, if in 1981 the expected rate of inflation was 11 percent and in 1992 it was 2 percent, the "real rate" of interest was unchanged at 3 percent. A problem with that argument is that inflation expectations are not readily measurable, so the real rate of interest cannot be readily derived. The level of interest rates is affected by many dynamic factors, including inflation expectations, Federal Reserve monetary policies, supply and demand for credit, and investor perceptions of credit risk.

THE MISSING LINK

Extensive studies of the assumed link between government deficits and "real" interest rates have generally found no significant relationship. A U.S. Treasury Department study of a 1965–1983 sample period concluded that "it would appear that over the sample examined high federal deficits have had at most a negligible effect in raising real interest rates."[5] And this in 1984 from the prominent New York banker Walter Wriston, then chairman of Citibank/Citicorp: "The fact is that, in looking at the empirical evidence, it is hard to validate the common assertion that big deficits cause high interest rates."[6] Similar conclusions were reached in a number of academic studies cited in a 1994 *National Journal* article, which surveyed expert opinion

on the alleged link between government deficits and private investment. Consider the following excerpts from that article:

> Economist Robert S. Chirinko of the University of Illinois
> (Urbana-Champaign) has surveyed some 75 years of studies on
> the question of what drives investment. He found, he said in
> an interview, that "there really isn't any" evidence that deficits
> curtail investment. . . .
>
> Also cutting against the grain is a new study by economist
> Steven M. Fazzari of Washington University in St. Louis. Fazzari
> looked at capital investments by major manufacturers from
> 1971–90 and found that investment was influenced quite a bit
> by a firm's sales and cash flow—and not much at all by interest
> rates. "So deficit cutting is not likely to stimulate investment
> through the interest rate channel," Fazzari said in an interview.
>
> In *The Misunderstood Economy* . . . Northwestern University
> economist Robert Eisner . . . argues that increased government
> savings resulting from deficit reduction steps may be more than
> offset by shrinkage in savings by households and businesses.
> Therefore, deficit reduction won't necessarily increase the total
> pool of savings available for investment. . . .
>
> Ohio State University economist Paul Evans, a self-described
> Republican conservative, has pored through data on budget
> deficits and interest rates during the 1980s and other periods,
> not only in the United States, but also in Canada, France, Ger-
> many, Japan and the United Kingdom. His conclusion? "You
> can pick your period, and you won't find any strong relationship
> between budget deficits and interest rates. . . . I really don't
> know exactly why," he said in an interview.[7]

We should not be surprised that these studies did not find a link
between government deficits and private investment. The surprise is
that so much effort was expended looking for that link; it never
existed and thus is not to be found. What's more, there is no logical
reason to assume the existence of such a link. The link between private
investment and the government's budget, if any, should logically be
found in an analysis of changes in the amounts and types of govern-

ment spending and tax revenues, not borrowing. It is the taxing and spending that redirects resources from private to public purposes. That should be self-evident.

Yet, as stated in that *National Journal* article, "Washington's conventional wisdom holds that reductions in the deficit lead to cuts in interest rates that lower the cost of capital for businesses and thereby boost investment." One reason to be nervous about this conventional wisdom is its implication that if Washington were to raise taxes to eliminate the deficit, it would also eliminate the crowding-out problem.

CROWDING OUT WITH A BALANCED BUDGET

Consider an extreme case of crowding out, not with a federal deficit but with a balanced budget. Let us assume that the government fills all the orders on the lobbyists' wish lists and thus increases government spending from the current 23 percent of gross domestic product to, say, 50 percent of GDP. Assume further that the government raises taxes to finance this additional spending and to eliminate the present deficit as well.

Presumably, the deficit hawks and the big spenders would both be happy: the budget would be balanced, and there would be ample funds for space exploration, military readiness, universal health care, the elimination of poverty, and resumption of long-delayed construction of and improvements to roads, bridges, and other public facilities throughout the country. All would be right with the world. Right? Wrong. That would be real crowding out of private spending and investment. The consequences would be disastrous for our economy and for our free-enterprise system.

The last time government spending rose to 50 percent of GDP was in World War II, but, as mentioned in chapter 2, the government knew better than to try to finance the war by increasing taxes. With the war financed largely by borrowing, the personal savings rate between 1940 and 1944 shot up from 4 percent to 25 percent of disposable personal income (compared with rates of 4 to 5 percent in the 1990s).[8] Even then, with a popular war and patriotism at a record high, it was necessary to impose a comprehensive system of wage and price controls, rationing (with black markets), and a virtual freeze on the production of many consumer goods, including new housing and automobiles. The economic reality was that approximately half of the labor force was producing guns, tanks, planes, and other goods and services (for the government) that it could not consume, so the alternatives were forced saving or runaway inflation.

People accepted the rigors of a wartime economy in part because of the national security threat but also because the hardships were viewed as temporary—"for the duration" was a common expression accompanying announcements of limitations on the availability of various consumer goods. But wars end. Somebody wins. What was acceptable for the duration of the war would not be acceptable in a time of peace.

It is naive to think that today we could have anything like half our workers producing public facilities, military equipment, or other goods and services that no one could consume at the time of production. What would they do with their paychecks? They would try to buy the consumer goods and services produced by the other half of the labor force. But the other half of the labor force would not adjust easily to such a reduction in their living standards as would be required by this increased competition for the fruits of their labor. So runaway inflation or rationing would be inevitable. So it was in wartime, and so it would certainly be in peacetime.

To be sure, the above is an extreme example, but the point should be clear: increased government spending is increased crowding out of private spending, no matter how it is financed.

CROWDING IN

If we were to accept the argument that government deficits crowd out private investment, then we might accept the argument that government surpluses "crowd in" private investment. By that logic, a tax increase resulting in a surplus would lead to an increase in private investment. The government takes more money from the private sector, and somehow the private sector has more money to save or invest. Nonsense.

On the other hand, we might logically expect that a reduction in government spending would lead to some crowding in of private investment—if the spending cutback resulted in reduced government demands for labor, materials, or other real resources and thus increased availability of those resources at lower prices to private investors.

No judgment is made here as to whether private investment is better than government investment. It depends on the purpose. There is a general presumption in our society in favor of private investment, but I have not heard anyone suggest that private investment in an illegal drug operation or a bordello would be better for society than government investment in a veterans hospital or a health clinic for poor children. My point is that people should not be ready to open their wallets to pay more taxes solely on the basis of the senseless political argument that government deficits crowd out private investment.

Shifting for a moment from economics to political science, which is more acceptable from a political standpoint—more government borrowing or more taxation? Former president George Bush was widely criticized during his failed reelection campaign in 1992 for having increased both taxes and the national debt. Would he have been less criticized had he not increased taxes but borrowed more? We will never know, but let's assume for the moment that borrowing is less subject to political discipline and is thus the greater evil. (Bush apparently never felt compelled to say, "Read my lips, no new borrowing.") Based on that assumption, it is of course better, from the standpoints of good budgeting and good economics, to tax than to borrow. Deficits should be curtailed to ensure greater reliance on upfront taxation, and thus discipline over spending and a more efficient allocation of economic resources.

CONCLUSION

To sum up, it is not the federal deficit or debt that crowds out private investment in our economy. Economic studies have failed to find a link between federal budget deficits and interest rates. It is government spending that competes with, and crowds out, private spending, regardless of whether that spending is financed by taxes or by borrowing.

Deficits should be reduced to ensure greater discipline over government spending, but if we accomplish deficit reduction by increasing taxes, the crowding-out problem remains and may well worsen.

Having concluded that we should reduce government deficits, what does this tell us about the government debt? Nothing. It's too late. As each annual deficit adds to the public debt, another horse is out of the barn. The undisciplined spending has already occurred.

One might argue that the debt must be reduced because the interest on the debt is now so large that it accounts for the entire budget deficit. That argument does not recognize the important differences between interest on the debt and other government spending, which is the subject of the next chapter.

4 Myth Number Three: The "Unsustainable" Interest Burden

In CHAPTER 1 we noted President Clinton's concern that the annual bill for interest on the public debt is becoming so big that there will not be enough money left in the budget to meet other critical needs. It is not clear whether this is an economic or a political judgment.

The president is certainly right on the numbers. Net interest outlays increased from $14.4 billion in fiscal year 1970 to $52.5 billion in fiscal year 1980, $184.2 billion in fiscal year 1990, and $232.2 billion in fiscal year 1995. (See table 10-1 for more information.)

The mounting interest payments on the federal debt surely have added to budget-balancing pressures to increase taxes or reduce spending for social programs (although in the 1995–1996 budget negotiations leaders of both political parties were proposing tax reductions). Yet so long as interest is included in the unified budget deficit, the budget will probably not be balanced, not in 2002 or 2010 or ever. The public debt interest is just too big. The political will for the needed tax increases or spending cuts is just too small. The budget has not been balanced since 1969, and neither political party in Congress is talking about a balance before 2002. That's one-third of a century of annual deficits, regularly punctuated by broken political promises to end them. The only difference between today's promises and yesterday's is that politicians used to claim that the budget would be balanced during their term in office; now they say it will be balanced during their successors' terms, seven to ten years down the line. That's incredible. No Congress can bind a successor Congress.

So the "goal" of balancing the federal unified budget is an illusion. Continued lip service to that goal will just add to public cynicism and further undermine what little confidence remains in the government's ability to manage its finances.

INTEREST HAS LITTLE ECONOMIC EFFECT

But these considerations are essentially political and should not be confused with economic considerations. From an economic standpoint, there is no unsustainable interest burden. Interest payments do not have significant effects on aggregate economic demand or, as indicated in chapter 5, on income redistribution in this country. So interest should not be likened to other federal spending. The public debt interest is not in itself a drain on economic resources; it is neither current government consumption nor investment. Unlike spending for military or social programs, interest payments do not directly affect the allocation of resources in our economy.

Consider the interest cost difference between debt financing and tax financing of a particular $100 million in government spending. In the case of tax financing, the private sector puts up the $100 million in cash and there is no public debt interest flow. In the case of debt financing, the private sector puts up the $100 million in cash but gets $100 million in Treasury securities.

Let's say the securities pay 8 percent interest, or $8 million a year. Then the private sector, with its taxpayer hat on, pays $8 million in additional taxes each year for this added interest on the public debt but also, with its investor hat on, receives an additional $8 million a year in interest income from the Treasury securities. So the annual flow of funds between the government and the private sector nets out, and the private sector is in essentially the same position as if the government spending were financed with taxes in the first place. If the $100 million in new Treasury debt is eventually retired, rather than refinanced, the private sector is paid back its $100 million, but it has to pay $100 million more in taxes to provide funds for the debt repayment.

The $100 million of spending will, of course, by its nature have certain effects on investment and consumption in the economy, regardless of whether it is financed by government borrowing or taxation. Either way, with debt or tax financing, the private sector is taxed to pay for the government spending. It could not be otherwise. Where else would the money come from? Yet our leaders bemoan the fact that interest on the public debt is estimated to become the largest single item in the federal budget by the end of this decade. Conservatives should say, "We should be so lucky!" Since interest on the public debt has little economic effect on the private sector, as interest rises relative to other government spending, which does consume economic resources, the relative burden of government spending on the private sector *declines*.

PRIVATE INTEREST VERSUS PUBLIC INTEREST

Why is there continued confusion on this point? Again, the problem seems to be a lack of recognition of the difference between personal and public finance. Interest payments are unquestionably a burden for the individual borrower, but in public finance we must take a collective view. We are paying the interest to ourselves. (The special case of interest payments to foreigners will be discussed in chapter 6.) We must look at society as a whole.

Should we conclude that interest on the public debt does not matter at all? No. We should not go that far, although some economists do. Consider the following statement by Abba Lerner, after his analysis of the alleged burden of the national debt: "This means that the absolute size of the national debt does not matter at all and that however large the interest payments that have to be made, these do not constitute any burden upon society as a whole."[1] Professor Lerner's statement does not recognize that interest payments on the public debt have some adverse effects, however marginal, including excessive interest payments to foreigners, since they are external to our "society as a whole"; uncertain internal income redistribution effects (although the analysis in chapter 5 suggests that those effects are much less than supposed); and impacts on private borrowers whose financial instruments carry interest rates tied to U.S. Treasury security yields. Also, as discussed in chapter 7, public debt interest adds to the Treasury's borrowing needs and, thus, to the government's increasingly dominant role in U.S. credit markets.

THE IMPACT OF INTEREST ON THE DEFICIT

In most of the post–World War II period, the inclusion of net interest in the federal budget deficit may have helped restrain federal spending. In fact, prior to the mid-1970s, exclusion of net interest from the deficit would generally have produced budget surpluses that might well have encouraged greater spending. Since the mid-1970s, however, total deficits have greatly exceeded net interest (see table 10-1). In the twenty year period, FY 1975–1994, the cumulative deficit ($3.1 trillion) exceeded cumulative net interest ($2.3 trillion) by $.8 trillion. The inclusion of interest in the deficit thus tended in the past two decades to mask the real deficit problem—the $.8 trillion that could have been controlled but was not.

Interest on the debt will continue to increase rapidly, as the debt itself increases. Net interest outlays increased from $85 billion in FY 1982 to $199 billion in FY 1992, even though market yields on Treasuries actually declined substantially. (As noted above, yields on three-year Treasuries declined from their peak of approximately 14 percent in 1981 to approximately 5 percent in 1992.)

Accordingly, Wall Street and a growing number of other observers recognize that so long as interest is included in the deficit calculations, the federal budget will probably never be balanced. This cynicism about deficit controllability will be even more widespread in the future, as it becomes increasingly evident that today's political promises to balance the budget early in the next century have no credibility.

THE POLITICS OF INTEREST

There is no financial or economic basis for the current notion of the Clinton administration that interest costs can be reduced by making changes in the way the public debt is managed. That notion is rooted in politics, not economics.

Of course, the federal budget is and always will be primarily a political document rather than a coherent economic plan or accounting statement. When I was a part of the economic forecasting staff of the Treasury, in the late 1950s and early 1960s, we were instructed to develop long-term forecasts, generally three, to cover a range of optimistic, moderate, and pessimistic outlooks. Then our political leaders would pick the alternative that produced a budget deficit or surplus of a size that was deemed to be politically correct. Why not? Economic forecasts were not that reliable anyway. Why burden the president with an unpopular budget presentation when there really isn't much confidence in the underlying economic assumptions, statistics, or forecasting techniques? Cynical? Perhaps, but that was the political reality. So far as I can tell the major difference today is that the computer speeds up the process and makes it easier to modify forecasts to satisfy the changing political imperatives of the day.

I do not mean to fault any particular president or political party for untruth in budgeting. Budget gimmickry is clearly a bipartisan sport. So I quote the following writer, Martin Armstrong, chairman of the Princeton Economic Institute, simply because he addresses the recent budget debate and reflects the current extreme level of cynicism about the budget process:

> When Bill Clinton announced that he would cut the deficit by a projected $500 billion over five years, . . . this miracle of miracles was accomplished in part by raising taxes $250 billion, but also via a parlor trick—shifting the funding of the national debt toward short-term maturities to save on interest expenditures.[2]

Mr. Armstrong then calculated that $250 billion of the projected deficit reduction was due not to a reduction in government but to an estimated interest savings from shortening the maturities of new government security issues. In fact, the actual amount of net interest savings claimed by the Clinton administration itself from its plan to "shorten maturity of debt securities" was $16.4 billion for the entire five-year period 1994–1998,[3] not the $250 billion claimed by Mr. Armstrong.

It is apparent from table 4-1 that longer-term offerings (issues with maturities of more than five years) are a very small portion of Treasury financing. The annual rate of new Treasury thirty-year bond issues had been about $48 billion in early 1992, when the Bush administration cut it back to about $40 billion. Then the Clinton administration cut it back by $18 billion to about $22 billion in 1993 and in 1994. In 1993 the Clinton administration also eliminated seven-year note issues, which had been running at about $40 billion a year. So Clinton's cutback on long-term financing was no more than $58 billion a year, and the annual interest savings from shifting to shorter-term financing could only be a small fraction of that amount.

Mr. Armstrong also noted that "Until the Clinton years, every administration since World War II tried to extend the national debt for as long as possible." Not true. As indicated above, the Bush administration had cut back on the thirty-year bonds in 1992. Before that, I was on the Treasury's debt management staff under every administration from Eisenhower through Reagan, and no administration sought to extend the debt for "as long as possible." No one was more committed to debt extension than I, but we never considered going so far as to eliminate short-term Treasury bills, for example, or to force-feed the market with thirty-year bonds at higher and higher interest rates just for the sake of more debt extension.[4] What we sought and achieved was a gradual development over many years of a cost-effective Treasury bond market by making incremental increases in the size of regular quarterly offerings of thirty-year bonds.

Yet Mr. Armstrong is right to say that the Clinton administration engaged in budget gimmickry. As a taxpayer, I was sickened when I heard about it. I had spent thirty-two years on the debt management staff at the Treasury and had never seen the management of the public debt so blatantly politicized. There was nothing clever about the particular political tactic employed by the Clinton administration. The same gimmick had been proposed to the Treasury many times before, under both Republican and Democratic administrations. It was just the same old simple-minded notion that the Treasury could

Table 4-1 Issues of U.S. Treasury marketable securities, fiscal year 1995 (billions of dollars)

Maturity	Frequency of issue	Oct–Dec	Jan–Mar	Apr–Jun	Jul–Sep	Total
Cash management bills[a]	As needed	35	31	59	23	149
13-week bills	Weekly	176	173	171	165	686
26-week bills	Weekly	178	174	175	169	696
52-week bills	Every 4 weeks	52	52	74	56	234
2-year notes	Monthly	38	77	57	38	210
3-year notes	Quarterly	21	21	21	22	86
5-year notes	Monthly	24	50	38	24	136
10-year notes	Quarterly	14	14	15	15	58
30-year bonds	Semiannually		12		13	24
Total		539	605	609	526	2279
Refundings		477	531	584	501	2093
Net borrowing		61	74	25	26	187

Source: U.S. Treasury Department, Treasury Bulletin, March 1995, June 1995, September 1995, and December 1995, Tables PDO-2 and PDO-3.

Note: U.S. savings bonds and other nonmarketable securities are excluded.

[a]Maturities ranged from 8 to 66 days in 1995.

reduce interest costs by issuing more short-term securities and fewer long-term securities, because short-term interest rates were generally lower than long-term interest rates.

That notion overlooks the fact that the level of interest rates is constantly changing. Interest rates are extremely volatile over the course of the business cycle, especially short-term rates.[5] For example, in 1993, when Clinton reduced the issues of thirty-year bonds and replaced them with short-term Treasury bills, interest rates for thirty-year bonds were about 6 percent and those for one-year Treasury bills about 3 percent. Replacing thirty-year bond issues with a like amount of one-year Treasury bill issues would thus appear to reduce borrowing costs for that issue amount by 50 percent. But one year later the level of market interest rates in the United States rose substantially; one-year rates went up to 6 percent and thirty-year rates to 8 percent. Thus Treasury missed the opportunity in 1993 to take full advantage of the historically low thirty-year bond rate, and in 1994 Treasury had to refinance its one-year bills at a much higher rate.

Other borrowers were not so foolish. They took advantage of the relatively low interest rates in 1993. For example, net corporate and foreign bond issues in the United States increased from $160 billion in 1992 to $253 billion in 1993 and then declined to $142 billion in 1994.[6] Individual homeowners rushed in droves to refinance their home mortgages and lock in the unusually low long-term mortgage interest rates. Only the U.S. Government went in the other direction and, incredibly, actually reduced its long-term borrowing and increased its short-term borrowing by a like amount.

The reasoning involved here is based on plain common sense. We are not talking about arcane high-finance strategy. The average American homeowner understands that shifting from a thirty-year, fixed-rate mortgage to a variable-rate mortgage with no cap on the amount by which interest payments might increase each year involves a sizeable risk that the homeowner may not be able to meet the increased mortgage payments. The variable-rate mortgage might be cheaper than the thirty-year, fixed-rate mortgage in the first year or two, but much more expensive thereafter. No one knows which is cheaper in the long run, and it takes thirty years to find out. Nonetheless, since long-term interest rates had declined in 1993 to levels not seen for twenty-five years, it was generally recognized, except by the Clinton administration, that it was not a good year to shift from long-term to short-term financing.

The government, like the average American homeowner or corporation, must consider its financial position in the long run. Indeed, while the average individual might have an investment horizon of no more than thirty years or so, the investment horizon of the government is infinite. President Clinton's investment horizon, however, may have been the 1996 election. If he's lucky, he may well be able to claim some short-term net savings, but he has absolutely no justification for counting these savings at this time, let alone his projected savings over the next five years. Any corporation that tried to do that would be disowned by its auditor.

A corporate CEO must act in the long-run interest of the corporation and the stockholders. Unfortunately, the CEO of our country only has to make it to the next election. The presidents for the next twenty-seven years will then pay the price for his mismanagement of the public debt. The great irony here is that Clinton is able to use this gimmick of cutting back on long-term bond financing and claiming future interest savings only because his predecessors, both Democrats and Republicans, had resisted the temptation to use it themselves (overlooking the relatively mild slip by George Bush in 1992). Instead, they had prudently built up the stock of long-term bonds that Clinton is now running down. Their legacy turned out to be a sort of political war chest for Clinton that he is now squandering. It will be left to his successors to repair the damage he has done to the management of the public debt.

Could it be that the Clinton administration knew more than Wall Street and the rest of the country about where interest rates were going—that rates were going down so it made sense to shift to short-term borrowing in 1993 and then issue long-term securities at the lower interest rates later? No. As indicated above, interest rates actually went up sharply in 1994, so the rest of the country guessed right and the government guessed wrong. But that's beside the point. For four essential reasons, the U.S. Treasury should never determine the maturities of its security issues based on guesses about the behavior of interest rates.

First, the government does not have the foggiest idea where interest rates are going, and it should not pretend that it does. Of course, the secretary of the Treasury and certain other government officials often have advance knowledge of market developments, economic statistics, and legislative, regulatory, or other government actions that may well affect interest rates; but these are short-term factors that have little or nothing to do with the course of interest rates in the long run. It would of course be highly inappropriate for the Treasury to alter its financing plans because of its "insider" knowledge of factors that might cause short-run changes in interest rates. That would totally confuse investors and would be contrary to the Treasury's objective of minimizing the market impact of its financings.

Second, if maturity selection were based on interest rate forecasts, there would seldom if ever be a good time, politically, to issue long-term bonds. It is generally politically unacceptable for the government to predict that interest rates are going up. Presidents are not fond of saying that adoption of their economic program will mean that the American people will have to pay higher interest rates. Presidents generally predict lower interest rates, which of course has the politically desired effect of lowering the estimated budget deficit.

Third, the public debt is so large, and thus so potentially disruptive of financial markets, that the only sensible way to minimize the financing costs is to have a regular and predictable schedule of maturity offerings. That way private market participants know what the Treasury is going to do, and they can make their own borrowing or investment plans accordingly. Market disruption is minimized, and the Treasury is able to borrow at a lower cost. What economists call "price discovery"—knowing the supply and demand factors that influence price—is improved. The playing field is more level.

This means smaller banks, fund managers, and other minor players are less vulnerable to the sharp practices of some of Wall Street's big players in the Treasury security auctions. This approach also discourages suspicion of favoritism, leaks of sensitive information about Treasury's borrowing plans, and unsound market speculation based on uncertainties created by the government itself. Investors hate uncertainty. Uncertainty is risk. Risk adds to cost, and thus to the cost to the taxpayer of financing the public debt. For these reasons, the Treasury should make its financing as predictable, even as dull, as possible.

Fourth, the Treasury should maintain a reliable, continuing presence in every maturity sector of the market, thereby ensuring broad demand for its securities and thus lower costs of borrowing. The market for short-term Treasury bills is entirely different from the market for two-to-ten-year Treasury notes or the market for thirty-year Treasury bonds. Each maturity has a special following, based on the many and varied special needs of a wide range of investors and other market participants throughout the world. Each market segment has to be carefully developed and nurtured. To drastically cut the supply of long-term securities and increase bill issues creates market uncertainty, undermines investor confidence in the management of the public debt, and thus adds to Treasury's borrowing costs. To do so for purely political reasons is irresponsible.

Throughout my career in the Treasury we were frequently pressured to eliminate or reduce the supply of long-term bond issues. Secretary of the Treasury George Humphrey was sharply criticized by members of Congress in 1953 for issuing thirty-year bonds at an interest rate of 3¼ percent, which at the time was viewed as outrageously high. That bond issue turned out to be one of the most successful Treasury financings, as market interest rates increased throughout the life of the bonds. When the bonds finally matured in 1983 they were refunded by the Treasury with new thirty-year bonds at an interest rate of 12 percent.

At times administration officials would try to get Treasury to cut back on long-term bonds because they found them politically embarrassing. They would make speeches proclaiming that the president's economic program was going to reduce interest rates, and a cynic in the audience would say, "If you are so sure of that, why are you still issuing long-term bonds at a higher cost now than later, when interest rates will supposedly be down?" Of course, there was no way of knowing when rates would come down, and the Treasury was not willing to put the taxpayers' money where the politicians' mouths were. Besides, once on that slippery slope of postponing bond issues until rates come down, it becomes politically difficult for the Treasury to reenter the bond market, since that reentry might be construed as a politically unpopular forecast that rates will be going up.

At other times when I worked at the Treasury, the Office of Management and Budget, in its frequent desperate searches for politically acceptable estimates of declining deficits, would run out of legitimate spending cuts and turn instead to wishful thinking in what became known as *rosy scenarios.* These included unrealistically low estimates of interest rates and Treasury borrowing costs, sometimes based on assumptions that Treasury would cut back on bond issues and borrow at lower interest rates in the short-term Treasury bill market.

While the bureaucratic fights, both inside and outside the Treasury, got pretty bloody, the Treasury managed to resist attempts to politicize debt management. Consequently, in my view, the Treasury earned the respect and confidence of financial market participants, which helped the president's political credibility much more than the momentary relief he might have gotten from underestimating the budget deficit. A grand irony here is that virtually every administration goes to great lengths to earn the confidence of Wall Street to get investors to accept lower interest rates. While Wall Street may be fooled for a while by budget gimmickry in the areas of national defense or social programs, it cannot be fooled for a minute in its own areas of expertise—the government securities market and interest rate forecasts. The Clinton administration apparently did not understand this, and the President's credibility in financial markets surely suffered.

But the deed is done, and Treasury debt management, once politicized, will probably never be the same. The only remedy now is to take public debt management out of harm's way by taking interest on the public debt out of the budget deficit. Then future presidents would be unable to gimmick the budget with phony interest rate forecasts or debt management tricks that wind up increasing the real costs to the American taxpayer. Then the budget focus and debate would properly be on government *program* costs, which, unlike interest, are controllable.

As noted above, the current trend toward greater dependence on short-term financing of the public debt will result in greater fluctuations in interest payments on the public debt. Thus federal expenditures, including interest, and deficits are less predictable and controllable. Removing interest from the deficit calculation may be the only way to restore effective discipline over federal spending.

THE UNCONTROLLABILITY OF INTEREST

It has often been said that "Nothing is certain except death and taxes." Yet in both cases timing is everything and is highly uncertain. If you are looking for certainty, look to interest on the public debt. Congress raises or lowers various taxes on short notice, sometimes on a retroactive basis. But Congress does not change the government's commitment to pay interest on outstanding Treasury obligations. That commitment is backed by the full faith and credit of the United States. The securities have specified interest rates that must be paid as scheduled to avoid default. Default is unacceptable, both economically and politically; it would destroy the superior credit standing of the U.S. government, both at home and abroad, and it would destroy the credibility of the sitting president. Financial markets dependent on Treasury securities for various investment and collateral purposes would be disrupted. The position of Treasury securities as the premier securities in international financial markets would be diminished, as would the prestige of the United States abroad. This is discussed further in chapter 10.

We have no choice but to pay the interest on Treasury's obligations. When such a large component of the federal budget is completely uncontrollable, we must question proposals to eliminate the deficit. We should focus on spending that *is* controllable, spending that we can do something about.

INTEREST IS NOT A PROGRAM

The president's budget now recognizes a distinction between federal expenditures for interest and other federal expenditures; it reports as an information item a budget deficit figure that excludes interest and that has been characterized as a "primary" budget deficit. Thus in fiscal year 1994, the total deficit of $203.2 billion consisted of net interest of $203.0 billion and a primary deficit of just $.2 billion. Then in fiscal year 1995 the total deficit of $163.9 billion was substantially smaller than net interest outlays of $232.2 billion, producing a primary *surplus* of $68.3 billion. A more meaningful designation of the so-called primary deficit might be the *controllable* or *economic impact* or *program* deficit. *Primary* is a relative term, but we need a term that emphasizes the difference in kind between interest and other expenditures. Because the focus should be on controlling government spending programs, my personal preference would be *program* deficit. Interest is clearly not a program.

Again, the reason for separate treatment of interest in the budget is not to make more room for other spending but to exercise a greater discipline over other spending and to restore credibility to the budget process. Since the only effective way to stem the growth of public debt interest—for political or other reasons—is to stem the growth of the public debt, the interest question should be addressed in the congressional debt limit process, not the budget process. This will be discussed in chapter 10.

CONCLUSION

The growing interest on the public debt is more a political problem than an economic one. Unlike other federal spending, interest payments do not directly affect the investment or consumption of real economic resources. The net interest cost to the American people is essentially the same for government expenditures financed with taxes as it is for expenditures financed with borrowing. Interest is also the only major federal expenditure that is completely uncontrollable.

Thus interest should not be included in the federal budget, the purpose of which should be to control federal spending. Interest on the federal debt should be treated like other federal debt transactions rather than in the budget in the Congressional debt limit process.

So long as interest is included in the budget, the budget will likely never be balanced, and there will be further deterioration in public confidence in the management of the government's finances. Promises to balance the budget early in the next century will soon give way to the same old political realities of taxing and spending that have brought us budget deficits in every year since 1969.

The inclusion of interest in the budget has encouraged misman- agement of the public debt and overly optimistic forecasts of interest rates to justify unrealistically low estimates of federal spending, defi- cits, and debt. Excluding interest from the deficit would help restore credibility to the budget process, ensure a greater focus on government program spending, and achieve an immediate balance in a new *pro- gram* budget.

5 Myth Number Four: The Inequitable Interest Burden

So LET'S MOVE ON TO THE NEXT MYTH: that interest on the federal debt is regressive, that is, that wealthy investors in Treasury securities are being paid interest from the taxes collected from average Americans.

IN THE INTEREST OF JOHN Q. PUBLIC

Table 5-1 shows that Treasury securities are, in fact, largely held by institutions for the benefit of middle-income people. Of the total federal debt of $5 trillion, $1.3 trillion is held by the Social Security, Civil Service Retirement, and other government trust funds. Of the remaining $3.7 trillion—the debt held by the public—47 percent is held by U.S. banks, insurance companies, pension funds, and other private domestic institutions, largely for the benefit of middle-income depositors, policyholders, pension beneficiaries, and shareholders; 23 percent is held by foreigners (largely foreign central banks); 10 percent is held by state and local governments; and 10 percent is held by our central bank, the Federal Reserve System. Only the remaining 9 percent is held by individuals, and most of that is in the form of U.S. savings bonds, which are especially designed for people with modest sums to invest. So the principal investor in U.S. Treasury securities is John Q. Public, not John D. Rockefeller.

Table 5-1   Estimated ownership of public debt securities held by the public, September 30, 1995 (billions of dollars)

Investor group	Amount	Percent of total
Total held by the public	3,654	100
Foreign and international	848	23
State and local governments	370	10
Federal Reserve banks	374	10
Commercial banks	295	8
Insurance companies	255	7
Corporations	224	6
Money market funds	64	2
Individuals		
Savings bonds	172	5
Other securities	138	4
Other investors	878	24

Source: Derived from U.S Treasury Department, *Treasury Bulletin,* December 1995, tables OFS-1, OFS-2.

FINDINGS OF A TREASURY STUDY

Notwithstanding the above facts, interest on the public debt continues to be viewed in Washington as another way the rich get richer and the poor get poorer. This was a political issue in the 1950s when I first joined the Treasury. I had hoped it was finally resolved in 1984, when the Treasury responded to a congressional request for a study of the issue. The study, which covers the period 1960–1984, concludes, "Thus we find no basis for the belief that interest payments on the public debt lead to greater inequality in the distribution of income."[1] The study includes a chart that compares the percentages of federal personal income taxes paid by people in various income groups in 1981 with the percentages of interest income to people in those same income groups. Figure 5-1 shows for 1992 essentially the same picture shown in the Treasury chart for 1981. As economists would put it, the distribution of interest income is more progressive than the distribution of the federal income tax burden.[2]

The curves on figure 5-1 are called Lorenz curves. They are often used to measure inequalities in distributions of income, wealth, and

Figure 5-1 Distribution of interest income and income taxes paid

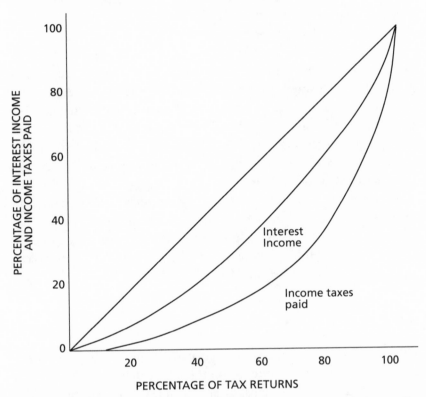

Source: Data from Internal Revenue Service, *Statistics of Income, 1992 Individual Income Tax Returns*. Figure is an update of a figure showing a similar picture of 1981 data in U.S. Treasury Department, "Ownership of and Interest Payments on the Public Debt," unpublished study, May 1984, chart 3.

Note: All percentages are classified by size of adjusted gross income.

tax burdens. In this case, we are comparing interest income and taxes paid, by income bracket, based on Internal Revenue Service data for 1992. The straight diagonal line represents perfectly equal distribution. The greater the departure from that line, the greater the inequality. The figure shows a greater equality in the distribution of interest income received than in income taxes paid.

Public debt interest is in fact far more democratic than the tax system. There are no political fingerprints on interest on the public debt; it is paid to those who choose to invest in Treasury securities for themselves or for the depositors, savers, or other beneficiaries they represent. By contrast, each new tax law is designed to benefit or cost a particular favored or disfavored constituency at the time.

As stated in the Treasury's 1984 study, "The data provide no evidence to support the suggestion that there is a significant class of people living off interest payments, whatever the source. Also, since the upper income groups pay more of the total personal income tax than they receive of total interest payments, the data does not support the thesis that there is a distributional effect from lower income groups to higher income groups because of an increase in the internal debt outstanding."[3]

Yet the myth persists. Senator Fritz Hollings, a Democrat from South Carolina, said, in arguing for a value-added tax (which has been criticized as regressive), "nothing is more regressive than interest costs."[4] Senator Hollings provided no facts to support his assertion; the Treasury study clearly refutes it.

ANATOMY OF A PHONY STATISTIC

Other Washington writers have cited statistics purporting to demonstrate the regressivity of interest on the public debt, but after further research found that the statistics demonstrated no such thing. Consider the following excerpt from an article in the *Postal Record,* a magazine published by the National Association of Letter Carriers (NALC), entitled "Interest Revisited":

> Interest on the national debt is the single biggest expense in the federal budget—in gross terms it costs more than Social Security. It is widely believed that this interest expense is regressive—that interest payments go to wealthy investors and are paid for by ordinary taxpayers. This is a myth.
>
> Unfortunately, this myth was perpetuated by Part 2 of the *Postal Record* series "A Working Person's Guide to the Economy" (see "Ten Things You Should Know About the Federal Budget" in the April 1993 issue).

That article repeated a statistic frequently bandied about in Washington budget debates: that the richest 10 percent of all Americans directly or indirectly hold nearly 85 percent of all outstanding Treasury securities. The problem is, this is not true. . . . [The article then cites statistics, similar to those in figure 5-1, showing that Treasury securities are held largely by institutions for the benefit of middle-class people.]

Letter carriers are a perfect example of middle-class ownership of the federal debt: the trust funds that finance their retirement benefits own a large share of the national debt and most of their Thrift Savings Plan accounts are invested in the G Fund, which buys U.S. Treasury securities.

The point is, interest on the national debt is much like other federal spending—it is paid for by and to the middle class, broadly defined. This is consistent with the larger point of Part 2 in the series: that contrary to public perception, federal spending largely involves the transfer of resources between groups of middle-class Americans.

Of course, there may be some regressivity involved within the middle class since not all American middle-class families have pension plans or mutual funds, but by and large, debt service is not regressive.

The *Postal Record* regrets the use of the inaccurate and misleading statistic—it was taken from another published source.[5]

The author of this NALC article, James W. Sauber, later sent me a letter in which he detailed his efforts to find the source of the phony statistic.[6] This was a classic example of how a Washington myth can be perpetuated.

The common image of "fat cat" rich investors living off the interest on the public debt is deeply rooted in American history. When I was a Treasury debt manager, one of my favorite office wall decorations was a framed cartoon from the *Harpers Weekly* issue of February 8, 1879. It depicted the joyous reactions of ordinary citizens to legislation authorizing the issuance of interest-bearing Treasury certificates in denominations as small as $10.[7] Americans of modest need were thus empowered to invest in their government's securities. The caption read, "New recruits to the Army of Bloated Bondholders. 'Let us hear no more about wiping out the Public Debt as with a Sponge.'" We've come a long way.

CONCLUSION

To sum up, there is no basis for the widely held view that interest on the public debt is paid to investors who are much wealthier than the average taxpayer, who gets stuck with the interest bill. In fact, Treasury securities are held largely by government and other institutional investors who hold them for the benefit of average, middle-income people. Indeed, the distribution of interest payments on the public debt appears to be much more democratic than the federal income tax system itself.

6 Myth Number Five:
The Foreign Threat

As to the alleged threat of growing dependence on foreign investors, their relative holdings of Treasury securities are no greater than they were in the late 1970s. At the end of fiscal year 1995 foreigners held 23 percent of total public holdings of Treasury securities, up from their 14 percent share in 1984 but just equal to their record 23 percent share in January 1979.[1]

THE NEED TO LOOK AT ALL INVESTMENTS

More important is the fact that foreign investment in Treasury securities is not in itself a matter of economic significance. What is significant is total foreign investment in the United States, not whether that investment is in the form of Treasury securities, federal agency securities, corporate securities, bank deposits, or other financial or real assets. If foreigners were to sell some of their Treasury securities and then purchase an equal amount of higher-yielding bonds issued by U.S. corporations, that would be of interest to Treasury debt managers and other market participants, but it should not be of interest to economists. Total foreign investment in the United States would not have changed.

Conversely, what if foreign investors were to make a portfolio decision to shift large sums out of U.S. bank deposits into U.S. Treasury bills? Let's say foreign holdings of Treasury bills doubled. Some observers might say the sky is falling, but there would still be no change in total foreign investment in the United States and thus no change of economic consequence to the United States. (Interest rates on Treasury securities might decline slightly in response to the added demand, and there might be some upward pressure on rates on bank deposits.)

As a Treasury debt manager I always welcomed foreign participation in our security auctions. It enabled us to get a higher price (lower interest rate) and save money for American taxpayers. The thought of discouraging this business always struck me as absurd. Should General Motors refuse to sell cars to foreigners?

THE NET FOREIGN INVESTMENT

Since most foreign investment in the United States is offset by U.S. investments abroad, the net foreign investment at the end of fiscal year 1995 was only about $900 billion, just 1.6 percent of total U.S. assets of $55 trillion, based on national wealth estimates compiled by the Office of Management and Budget in the fiscal year 1997 budget (see table 2-1). What threat can there be of foreign dominance when 98.4 percent of the nation's wealth is owned by Americans?

Even if foreigners increased their net investments in the United States substantially, it would not be rational to assume that the country would be worse off. The United States has chronic balance-of-payments deficits with the rest of the world because it imports more goods and services than it exports. So we pay foreigners more dollars for imports than they use to purchase our exports. The remaining dollars, the U.S. current account deficit, must be invested in U.S. physical or financial assets. (What else could foreigners do with the dollars?) Consequently, the United States is a net debtor nation, as it has been since 1987. Does the fact that we are a net debtor nation pose some sort of new threat to the Treasury securities market? No. As indicated above, foreigners held just as high a percentage of Treasury securities back in 1978, long before the United States became a net debtor nation. What about a threat to our economy? No. Additional foreign investment helps to provide new job opportunities for Americans, which may offset job losses that might result from the excess of imports over exports. The threat to our economy is not that foreigners invest in our country, it's that we do not save and invest enough ourselves.

THE SUPREMACY OF THE U.S. DOLLAR

Most foreign holdings of U.S. Treasury securities are a reflection of the strength of the U.S. economy. The United States is in a unique position in that its dollar is the major international reserve currency. As foreign central banks and other official institutions acquire U.S. dollars, they invest them in U.S. Treasury securities. At the end of fiscal year 1995, foreign central banks and other official institutions held 55 percent of the total of U.S. Treasury securities held by foreigners.[2]

Nearly half of all international trade is priced in dollars, and the dollar is involved in more than 40 percent of the world's foreign exchange transactions. In 1993, 44 percent of the investments throughout the world in stocks, bonds, bank deposits, and other financial instruments was denominated in dollars.[3]

The dollar-denominated U.S. Treasury security is the premier security in international financial markets, and there never has been any question of the financial ability of the United States to make good on its obligations.[4] As stated by economist Alan S. Blinder, who later became vice chairman of the Board of Governors of the Federal Reserve System, "As long as our borrowing is denominated in dollars, we never need fear defaulting for we can always print as many dollars as we need."[5]

WINNERS AND LOSERS

Yet the myth persists. Net foreign investment in the United States, especially by Japan, continues to be viewed as some sort of threat to the nation. As noted recently by Nobel Prize–winning economist Milton Friedman, "The rhetoric about our balance of payments deficit with Japan—whether in the print media, on television or in statements by the president or other prominent individuals—almost invariably treats the deficit as good for Japan and bad for us. I submit that the truth is almost the opposite. The deficit has been good for the United States. It has presumably been good for Japan as well, but that is much less clear, and, on net Japan may have lost."[6]

Friedman went on to explain that Japan may have been the loser because "many Japanese investments in the United States turned out to be duds." The Japanese went on an enormous shopping spree here in the late 1980s and early 1990s, buying up New York skyscrapers, California golf courses, and other real estate and business enterprises throughout the country, as well as U.S. Treasury and other securities. Americans were happy to sell real estate because the Japanese were willing to pay more than anyone else. As it turned out, the Japanese overpaid for many of these properties and suffered substantial losses later.

Many Americans were embarrassed to hear that the Japanese were buying up American cultural landmarks, like New York's Rockefeller Center in 1989, as if somehow the center could be moved to Japan. It was a blow to American pride—a symbol of Japanese economic superiority in the 1980s. As it turned out, it was the Japanese Mitsubishi Estate Company that lost face. The Manhattan commercial real estate market crashed a few years later, and in 1995 the Rockefeller Center went bankrupt. As reported in the *Wall Street Journal*, "To Mitsubishi's profound embarrassment, its purchase had become a prime example of how Japanese trophy hunters had wildly overpaid for American real estate."[7]

Another much-publicized blow to American pride was the 1990 sale of the famed Pebble Beach Golf Links in California to a Japanese developer for $841 million. Yet it was the Japanese that lost face (and money) when the developer's bank took over the Pebble Beach property in 1992 and sold it at a substantial loss for $500 million.[8]

While American investors in commercial real estate also suffered great losses, the Japanese losses have been compounded in recent years by the steady decline in the value of the American dollar relative to the Japanese yen.

Even if the Japanese had profited from their investments in the United States, that should not have been viewed as bad for the United States. Indeed, just the opposite view is held by economists from both ends of the political spectrum. As the conservative Milton Friedman said in an earlier writing, "It is a mystery to me why . . . it is regarded as a sign of Japanese strength and American weakness that the Japanese find it more attractive to invest in the U.S. than Japan. Surely it is precisely the reverse—a sign of U.S. strength and Japanese weakness."[9] And this from the well-known liberal economist Robert Heilbroner: "Owning a fraction of a nation's debt does not convey any special leverage to the holder; it may, in fact, make the creditor a hostage to the debtor's fortunes."[10]

Perhaps the more realistic view, which is a fundamental precept of free trade, is that foreign investment is generally a win-win situation. Surely, when U.S. corporations, such as McDonald's or Coca-Cola, invest in fast-food restaurants or bottling facilities in foreign countries, such investments are generally viewed as good for the United States and good for the foreign countries. The same should be true when the investment flows in the other direction, say, for the construction of a Japanese automobile assembly plant in the United States.

What about the oft-expressed concern that someday the Japanese will cut back on their U.S. investments? We had some experience with that in 1995, and the result was a decline in the value of the dollar relative to the Japanese yen. As reported in the *Washington Post:*

> What Japanese exporters earn each year by selling goods abroad is about $130 billion more than Japanese importers pay to foreign producers. For years, the extra dollars were invested in the United States or swapped for other currencies and invested elsewhere. Now, much of that money is returning home. Large losses on real estate deals, the stock market, overseas investments and bank loans have created a financial crisis in Japan. To cover some of those losses and provide funds to businesses unable to get bank credit, foreign earnings are being exchanged for yen, pushing up the Japanese currency's value.[11]

Of course, as the Japanese sell dollars and the dollar depreciates further relative to the yen, the Japanese lose more on their remaining U.S. investments.

Apart from these broad economic considerations, should we be concerned, from the narrow standpoint of Treasury debt management, about other countries owning our government's securities? Might they suddenly stop buying our securities or suddenly dump their holdings on the open market and cause a price drop that would mean higher interest rates for the U.S. Treasury on its new security issues?

Actually, foreign ownership of Treasury securities is spread over a large number of countries. The investment behavior of any one country is not likely to have a major impact on our government securities market. As of December 1994, the major holder, Japan, held $175 billion of Treasuries, which is less than the average volume of daily trading in the Treasury market. Only three countries—Japan, the United Kingdom, and Germany—held more than 1 percent of the Treasury debt in the hands of the public (see table 6-1). Also, if

Table 6-1　Foreign holdings of U.S. Treasury securities, December 31, 1994

Country	Holdings ($ billions)	As a percent of total Treasury securities held by the public
Japan	$175.4	5.0%
United Kingdom	91.0	2.6
Germany	54.5	1.5
Switzerland	32.4	0.9
Spain	27.9	0.8
Netherlands Antilles	27.8	0.8
Taiwan	25.8	0.7
OPEC	25.7	0.7
Canada	24.6	0.7
Singapore	21.9	0.6
Mainland China	20.5	0.6
Hong Kong	13.8	0.4
Belgium	13.1	0.4
France	9.7	0.3
Mexico	7.9	0.2
Other	116.6	3.3
Total	688.6	19.4

Source: U.S. Treasury estimates based on Treasury Foreign Portfolio Investment Survey benchmark as of end-year 1989 and monthly data collected under the Treasury International Capital reporting system.

foreigners were to sell amounts of Treasury securities so large that they could have a significant price effect, they presumably would do it carefully over a period of time to avoid driving down the price to the point where they would themselves suffer large losses. Finally, as noted above, 55 percent of foreign holdings of Treasury securities are held by foreign central banks, rather than by speculators or other private investors who would be more inclined to rush to sell their securities under volatile market conditions.

CONCLUSION

To conclude, the fact that foreigners hold a significant volume of U.S. Treasury securities should not be viewed as a problem. The Treasury clearly benefits from this added demand for its securities.

Our focus should be on net foreign investment in the United States, not whether that investment is in Treasury securities, corporate bonds, bank deposits, real estate, or other investments. The United States has indeed become a net debtor nation in recent years, but the amount of the net debt is relatively small compared with the wealth of this nation. Also, the net investment of foreigners in the United States may well be a net benefit to the U.S. economy rather than a burden.

7 The Federal Preemption of Credit Markets

Now for the bad news. In the previous chapters I have attempted to show that there is little basis for the concerns over the national debt as expressed by our political leaders. To tell the whole truth about the national debt, however, I must now focus on a major, related problem that is virtually ignored by those same politicians—that is, the impact of the federal government's total debt activities on U.S. credit markets.

A measure of that impact appears in the documents accompanying the president's annual budget submission to Congress. The measure shows how much of the net new borrowing (borrowing net of repayments) in the U.S. credit markets each year is required to finance the programs of the federal government. Thus it shows the combined impact of new federal borrowing (which is included in the national debt) and federally assisted borrowing (which is not included in the national debt).

Federally assisted borrowing includes government-guaranteed borrowing, such as loans insured by the Federal Housing Administration or guaranteed by the Small Business Administration; borrowing by government-sponsored enterprises (GSEs), such as Fannie Mae (formerly known as the Federal National Mortgage Association), the Farm Credit System, and the Student Loan Marketing Association; and mortgage-backed securities guaranteed by the Government National Mortgage Association and other federal housing agencies.

In fiscal year 1995 net federal borrowing from the public was $171.3 billion, net guaranteed borrowing was $26.2 billion, and net borrowing by GSEs was $158.3 billion. So the total of federal and federally assisted borrowing was $355.8 billion, which was 49.6 percent of total net borrowing in credit markets by domestic nonfinancial sectors of our economy (see table 7-1).[1] That is, after netting out all debt transactions among federal, federally guaranteed, and government-sponsored entities, the net market financing for these federal programs required 49.6 percent of the total credit extended to governments, businesses, households, and foreigners in U.S. credit markets.

There has been a dramatic increase in this federal share of total U.S. credit (see figure 7-1), from an average of 17 percent of net credit market borrowing in the 1960s to 27 percent in the 1970s and 41 percent in the 1980s.[2] In the five years 1991–1995, the average was an extraordinary 71 percent. (The peak was 89 percent in 1992.)[3] We have reached a point where most of the securities available to private investors in the United States are direct or indirect obligations of the federal government. What does this mean? Are the credit markets in the United States now largely nationalized . . . federalized . . . socialized, if you will? Does anyone care?

THE QUIET TAKEOVER

While these numbers appear in the president's budget documents every year, they get little attention from economists, the media, or politicians in the annual budget debates. Network TV is obsessed with government deficits and the federal debt. Yet there is virtually no mention of the borrowings by the GSEs or for the federal loan guarantee programs, which are financed largely outside the budget and are not included in the federal debt. (The only federal credit aids reflected in the federal debt are the $163 billion of government direct loans, discussed in chapter 3.) The federal government's takeover of the U.S. credit markets in recent years must be the biggest and quietest takeover in the country's financial history.

William Simon was the first secretary of the Treasury to call attention to the government's preempting of this growing share of

Table 7-1 Federal participation in U.S. credit market, fiscal years 1965–1995 (dollar amounts in billions)

Fiscal year	1965	1970	1975	1980	1985	1990	1991	1992	1993	1994	1995
Total net borrowing in U.S. market[a]	66.7	87.9	169.7	336.3	826.5	722.3	502.0	540.8	578.5	618.4	717.5
Federal borrowing from the public	3.9	3.5	51.0	69.5	199.4	220.8	277.4	310.7	247.4	184.7	171.3
Guaranteed borrowing	5.0	7.8	8.6	31.6	21.6	40.7	22.1	19.7	–2.0	38.7	26.2
GSE borrowing	1.2	4.9	5.3	21.4	57.9	115.4	124.6	150.8	170.2	140.0	158.3
Total federal and assisted borrowing	10.1	16.2	65.0	122.5	278.9	376.9	424.1	481.2	415.6	363.4	355.8
Federal percent[b]	15.1	18.4	38.3	36.4	33.7	52.2	84.5	89.0	71.8	58.8	49.6

Source: Office of Management and Budget, *Analytical Perspectives, Budget of the United States Government, Fiscal Year 1997* (Washington, D.C.: GPO, 1996), 198.

[a]Includes federal and federally assisted borrowing as well as unassisted borrowing by state and local governments, businesses, households, and foreigners in U.S. credit market.
[b]Federal and federally assisted borrowing as a percent of total net borrowing in U.S. credit market.

Figure 7-1 Share of credit market required to finance federal programs

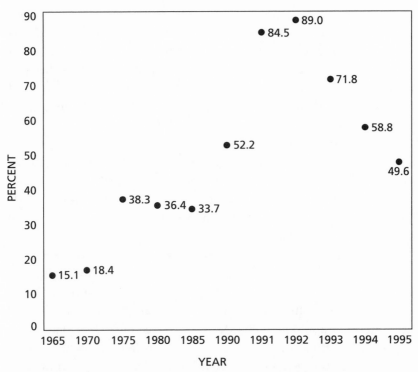

Source: Adapted from the Office of Management and Budget, *Analytical Perspectives, Budget of the United States Government, Fiscal Year 1996* (Washington, D.C.: GPO, 1995), 197.

Note: Market share is measured by net borrowing to finance federal programs (direct federal borrowing, federally guaranteed borrowing, and borrowing by government-sponsored enterprises) as a percentage of net funds raised in U.S. credit market.

the credit markets. He frequently expressed deep concerns about it in his testimony before Congress on the public debt limit and other matters in the mid-1970s. I recall hearing that Democratic Senator William Proxmire of Wisconsin, then chairman of the Senate Banking, Housing, and Urban Affairs Committee, said that "Simon has everyone scared up here." Given the subsequent explosive growth in federal and federally assisted borrowing activities, it seems Congress was not scared enough.

The Republican sponsors of the Contract with America go ballistic over government regulation of private business, but apparently have no problem with the government's actually usurping the functions of private business—in this case, the shifting of private credit risk from investors and private financial institutions to the federal taxpayer. The apparent explanation for the lackadaisical attitude toward this socialization of credit is that private lenders do not complain about it to their friends in Washington. They are just as happy as they can be, profiting from the business of providing credit effectively secured by Uncle Sam without having to take the risk normally associated with such profits.

The housing industry, the principal beneficiary of federally assisted credit, loves it. All the players—developers, builders, homeowners, realtors, lenders, investment bankers, investors, furniture and appliance store owners, and many others—welcome the reduced costs of housing finance and the shifting of private credit risks to the general taxpayer.

The principal sources of this largess, Fannie Mae and the Federal Home Loan Mortgage Corporation (FHLMC), commonly known as Freddie Mac, are politically powerful institutions with combined lending—which is financed largely with guaranteed mortgage-backed securities—of approximately $1.4 trillion (see table 7-2). The larger of the two, Fannie Mae, ensconced in its palatial headquarters on upper Wisconsin Avenue in Washington (but exempt from D.C. income taxes), is one of the most feared lobbies in town.

These government-sponsored enterprises have the best of both worlds: the pay and perks of giant private corporations and the monopoly, subsidies, and security of government agencies. Although arrangements vary among the GSEs, generally they are authorized to seek loans or other financial support from the Treasury, they are exempt from certain state and local taxes, and their securities are treated as if they were federal securities for various collateral, investment, and regulatory purposes.

Treasury Secretary Simon, who had a strong Wall Street background in the financing of sponsored enterprises, such as Fannie Mae, understood the political realities of congressional support for housing. In the mid-1970s I was asked to review a document prepared for Secretary Simon that discussed the role of the government in support-

Table 7-2   Federal and federally assisted borrowing from the
public, fiscal year 1995 (billions of dollars)

Borrower or guarantor entity	Net borrowing in year	Outstanding end of year
Federal agencies[a]	171.3	3,603.4
Government-sponsored enterprises (GSEs)	158.3	1,661.0
Fannie Mae	73.9	836.8
Federal Home Loan Mortgage Corporation	21.0	568.7
Federal Housing Finance Board	63.0	264.6
Farm Credit System	3.3	56.8
Student Loan Marketing Association	2.0	51.7
Adjustments to avoid double counting[b]	−5.0	−117.6
Guaranteed loans	26.2	726.8
Housing and Urban Development	38.2	869.9
Veterans Affairs	−2.9	154.5
Agriculture	−6.4	15.3
Education	9.5	86.1
Export-Import Bank	1.0	17.7
Small Business Administration	3.8	26.4
Other[c]	1.9	20.7
Adjustments to avoid double counting[d]	−18.9	−463.8
Total federal and assisted borrowing	355.8	5,991.2

Source: Office of Management and Budget, *Analytical Perspectives, Budget of the United States Government, Fiscal Year 1997* (Washington, D.C.: GPO, 1996), 160–165, 189.
[a]U.S. Treasury debt and minor amounts of other agency debt.
[b]Includes net GSE debt transactions with other GSEs, federal agencies, and federally guaranteed borrowers.
[c]Includes loans for international development, foreign military sales, overseas private investments, and ship financing.
[d]Government National Mortgage Association guarantees of mortgage-backed securities to finance insured housing loans.

ing Fannie Mae and the investors in Fannie Mae's securities. I pointed out that, legally, Fannie Mae's debt was not guaranteed by the government (although the Treasury was authorized to lend to Fannie Mae, and investors viewed this as government protection against a Fannie Mae default). When the document came back with Secretary Simon's scribbled comments in the margin, I saw that he had likened my comments to the droppings of bulls. I was, of course, technically correct; but Simon was right. He recognized that, as a practical political matter, Fannie Mae trades on the Treasury's credit.

While there were some raised eyebrows when a retiring CEO of Fannie Mae, David O. Maxwell, floated away in a $27 million golden parachute,[4] there has been no serious challenge to such extraordinary compensation or to other special privileges and benefits enjoyed by sponsored-enterprise executives. These are the new princes of American finance, living not by their entrepreneurial wits but by the grace of the state. There is something wrong with a system where a federal bureaucrat, the chairman of Fannie Mae, was paid $4.4 million in 1994, which was more than the combined salaries of the president of the United States and his entire cabinet.

Why should we be concerned about the growth of the GSEs and other federal credit assistance programs? One concern is the cost to the Treasury, and thus to the taxpayer, from the competition with the GSEs and guaranteed borrowers in the government securities market. When the Treasury is perceived as prepared to stand behind similar debt securities issued by the GSEs, the GSE securities become close substitutes for Treasury securities in the portfolios of many investors. Thus the Treasury must pay a somewhat higher interest rate on its own borrowings.

The situation is somewhat analogous to that of a person who cosigns the loan of a friend or relative and later finds that he must pay a higher interest rate on his own subsequent borrowings because the cosigned loan increased his contingent liabilities. When you lend your credit standing to someone else you may diminish its value to yourself. While the Treasury's creditworthiness is not diminished, its borrowing advantage is. As shown in table 7-2, GSE debt totals $1.7 trillion, 46 percent as much as the marketable Treasury debt of $3.6 trillion. (If the Treasury were to increase its direct debt in the market by 46 percent, it would clearly have to pay a higher interest rate.) Even if the competition from GSE debt added only one one-hundredth of 1 percent to Treasury's average cost of borrowing (for example, an increase from 6.00 percent to 6.01 percent), the annual interest cost on the government's marketable debt would increase by $360 million.

Another obvious concern is the potential cost to the government from losses on guaranteed loans and GSE losses, which would lead to demands on the Treasury for financial assistance to the GSEs.

Also, the subsidy elements in certain government-assisted loans can have significant effects on the allocation of credit resources. Some loans, such as those for low-income or public housing, have been so heavily subsidized as to be like outright government grants in their economic effects. But many federal credit programs, such as those for moderate income housing, cost the government little and may have only marginal economic impacts.

Since federally assisted credit is largely for private investment in housing, and is also supportive of small business, education, agriculture, and many other private investment areas, it may be viewed as facilitating rather than crowding out private investment. The critical question is whether the right type of private investment is being encouraged by these federal credit programs. Are we diverting too many real resources to, for example, housing and agriculture at the expense of other, perhaps more productive areas of the economy?

THE THREAT TO CREDIT QUALITY

The major concern with the shifting of credit risk from the private sector to the government is the loss of market discipline usually relied on to maintain the quality of credit. Private lenders, who are normally bound to exercise due diligence through careful inspections, appraisals, and credit investigations before extending credit, have less incentive to be so diligent when the government is guaranteeing them against loss. The old rules of "know your customer" and "know your collateral" are relaxed. To an increasing degree the "customer" is now Uncle Sam, not the borrower, and the ultimate "collateral" is the Treasury's taxing power, not the property that is supposedly securing the loan. A resulting decline in the quality of credit could lead to defaults and weaknesses in the national financial structure during periods of economic stress.

Government guarantees are too often perceived as eliminating risk, which they do for the guaranteed lender but not for the economy. To be sure, the spreading of risk through private insurance institutions, based on sound actuarial analysis, is vital to a growing economy. But generally the justification for granting government guarantees is to facilitate activities that are not insurable or "bankable," that is, would not meet the test of the private market.

These high-risk activities are the very ones that should be subject to the most careful credit investigations and appraisals. Yet because of the government guarantees, lenders have less, rather than more, incentive to devote their credit evaluation resources to such activities. Government guarantees, rather than reducing or shifting risk, actually add risk to the economy.

I am not suggesting that the government should not take risks. There are many successful loan guarantee programs. The most cited example of a good government guarantee program is the FHA single-family mortgage insurance program, which has generally been self-supporting since its inception in the 1930s and has served as a model for private lenders in making long-term, low-down-payment loans without a government guarantee. Even in loan guarantee programs with high defaults, such as student loans, the public benefits may well exceed the costs.

On the other hand, perhaps the greatest example of a government guarantee program gone wrong is the excessive risk creation from federal deposit insurance for savings and loan associations (which is not included in the government's measure of federally assisted credit). The catastrophic failure of savings and loan associations (S&Ls) in the early 1980s, which cost the government an estimated $180 billion (not the $500 billion claimed by some critics), was due in large part to the government deposit insurance.[5] At that time the insurance was irresponsibly increased from $40,000 to $100,000 for each individual account, and the lending powers of the S&Ls were broadened. The S&Ls would not have been able to make the questionable loans that led to their failure had it not been for excessive government insurance. That insurance increase led to a bidding war by S&Ls for the so-called hot money, or brokered deposits, of large depositors throughout the country who had little incentive to question the unsound lending practices of the S&Ls. S&Ls paid higher and higher interest rates to attract short-term deposits to finance their holdings of longer-term loans made earlier at lower rates. Many were transformed from their traditional role as thrift institutions invested in relatively safe home mortgages to aggressive financiers of highly speculative commercial development projects.

Many complex economic and political factors led to the demise of the S&Ls, but the excessive government guarantees were clearly a principal cause. As stated by the Congressional Budget Office, "Most experts agree that the existence of the federal deposit insurance system and the way in which regulators operated it were major culprits in the thrift crisis."[6] The point was made more forcefully by a well-known expert, Edward Kane, in *The S&L Insurance Mess: How Did It Happen?*:

> An apt name for these insolvent, hellbent-for-leather thrifts is institutional zombies. The economic life they enjoy is an unnatural life-in-death existence in that, if they had not been insured, the firms' creditors would have taken control from stockholders once it became clear that their enterprises' net worth was exhausted. In effect, a zombie has transcended his natural death from accumulated losses by the black magic of federal guarantees.[7]

Thus, the idea of deposit insurance, put into effect in the 1930s to protect the person with a relatively small savings account and to encourage homeownership, was corrupted by political catering to powerful S&L lobbies.

The S&L disaster is a dramatic showing of how excessive government guarantees can lead to a fatal loss of market discipline in the allocation of credit. The debt securities available to private investors are now largely direct or indirect obligations of the federal government. That is the most serious issue raised by the federal government's recent preemption of the bulk of the credit flows in our economy.

THE ROAD TO REFORM

I should note that recent growth has been largely in direct federal borrowing and sponsored-enterprise borrowing rather than in guaranteed borrowing. In the five-year period 1991–1995, net federal borrowing was $1,192 billion, net sponsored-enterprise borrowing (the fastest growing area) was $744 billion, and net guaranteed borrowing was just $105 billion.[8] Considerable progress has been made in recent years in rationalizing the financing and budget control of federal loan guarantee programs. This progress is due largely to two pieces of "good government" legislation, the Federal Financing Bank Act of 1973 and the Federal Credit Reform Act of 1990, as I'll explain shortly.

During my three decades in the Treasury hardly a month went by that I was not fighting (in a largely losing battle) some proposal to extend the Treasury's credit to yet another sector of the economy through some sort of "off-budget" program of government guarantees, insurance, or direct loans by a new lending entity. Every major program agency provides some form of credit assistance to its constituency . . . housing, agriculture, small business, transportation, education, foreign aid, community development, utilities, and many others. Prior to 1973, most of these credit aids were financed with some sort of government-backed securities issued in the private market so they would not have to be included in the politically sensitive federal budget expenditures; this in turn excluded them from any accounting in the direct federal debt.

The major problems created by these "off-budget" guaranteed securities were (1) the cost of financing was higher, compared with direct loans financed by Treasury borrowing, because private investors demanded far higher interest rates on these fully guaranteed securities than on Treasury securities, which were more liquid and better established in the market; and (2) the programs financed with these guaranteed securities, since the expenditures were outside the budget, were out of control.

To deal with these problems, in the late 1960s I proposed the establishment of a Federal Financing Bank (FFB), which would permit the Treasury to act as an intermediary to consolidate the financing of the various agency-guaranteed securities. Then Under Secretary of the Treasury Paul Volcker (later chairman of the Board of Governors of the Federal Reserve System) provided the leadership in gaining White House and congressional approval of the proposal. Essentially, the FFB, although nominally a bank and a lending institution, was a mechanism to permit the Treasury to purchase agency-guaranteed securities without changing their off-budget status. Otherwise, the securities would have gone into the marketplace at interest rates much higher than the rates on the Treasury securities sold to purchase them.

Under Secretary Volcker presented the FFB proposal as a federal debt management measure that would reduce the costs to government, and to certain assisted borrowers, of financing loan guarantee programs. The FFB was not presented as a reform measure to curb the growth of loan guarantee programs, but it was clear that the FFB would have that potential. It would expose many "loan guarantee" programs for what they already functionally were—direct loan programs financed in the securities markets with the government's credit to avoid the discipline both of the budget and of the marketplace.

The FFB proposal got mixed reviews on Wall Street. Some investment bankers, including William Simon, who was then at Salomon Brothers, applauded the FFB because it saved money for the government and rationalized the financing of government loan guarantee programs. Salomon Brothers and several other large investment banking firms had been earning substantial fees from the development and marketing of various forms of government-guaranteed securities. Because the FFB eliminated the need for those investment banking services, many of Simon's colleagues did not share in his expression of public-spirited support.

I recall a visit from one irate investment banker who said the FFB was socialized credit. He did not appreciate my response, which was that the socialization of credit occurred when the government guaranteed the ostensibly private securities, thus assuming the risks that the private market would normally assume in a free-market economy. The FFB would rid the market of such guaranteed securities and reduce the cost to the taxpayer of such socialized credit.

The FFB was established in the Federal Financing Bank Act of 1973 and soon became the largest "lending institution" in the nation, with billions of dollars of savings in the interest costs of financing federal loan guarantee programs. Initially, the FFB did not change the off-budget status of the guarantee programs (that would have been politically impossible at the time), but it made them more visible as compared with the various complicated mechanisms used by the program agencies to secure off-budget financing in the market. Eventually this new visibility led to greater understanding of these programs and to the inclusion of FFB-financed loans in the budget. It also led to the enactment of a requirement in the Federal Credit Reform Act of 1990 (which was initially drafted by Treasury staff in 1986)[9] to include in the budget the estimated present value of costs to government from interest rate and other subsidies in new loans made under both direct and guaranteed loan programs. Thus the budget incentive to use loan guarantees—rather than more efficient and controllable direct loans—was eliminated, and the need for the FFB declined.[10]

It took more than two decades, but the Treasury's original objectives—reducing the financing costs of federal credit programs and ensuring greater budget controls over these programs—were both achieved.

No such progress can be claimed in the area of government-sponsored enterprises. While there has been much discussion of the need to reduce the subsidy to GSEs, for example, by removing their special tax advantages or their financial backing from the Treasury, nothing has been done. The GSEs' popularity with Congress has insulated them from any effort to initiate significant reform.

As this book goes to the printer, federal agencies have not yet completed long-overdue studies on the privatization of Fannie Mae and Freddie Mac. Legislation enacted in October 1992 required that the General Accounting Office, HUD, the Treasury, and the Congressional Budget Office each conduct and submit by October 1994 a study "regarding the desirability and feasibility of repealing the Federal charters of the Federal National Mortgage Association and the Federal Home Loan Mortgage Corporation, eliminating any Federal sponsorship of the enterprises, and allowing the enterprises to continue to operate as fully private entities."[11] (The studies are expected to be completed in the summer of 1996.)

The GSEs continue to be neither fish nor fowl—privately owned but federally sponsored. They remain wards of the state, but very rich wards indeed. They lack accountability. They should be subject either to the discipline of the free competitive market or to the budgetary or other disciplines imposed on other government agencies.

If it is determined that, after decades of experimentation (Fannie Mae and Freddie Mac, the largest GSEs, were established as private entities in 1970), the GSEs cannot stand on their own feet in the market, we should look at other approaches that would reduce their costs to the government and permit private financial institutions to fully compete with the GSEs.

An effective way to accomplish this would be to charge the GSEs guarantee or user fees, which would offset their advantage over competing private institutions that are self-supporting. For example, if average borrowing costs were 7 percent for the GSEs, because the government backing gave them an AAA rating, and 8 percent for similar but self-supporting institutions with an A rating, a guarantee fee of 1 percent would level the playing field. Such fees should be deposited in the Treasury (1) to compensate for the additional borrowing costs incurred by the Treasury in competing with Treasury-backed GSE securities in the market and (2) to provide a reserve against possible losses to the Treasury from any future direct financial assistance to the GSEs.

A good first step is the following 1996 recommendation of the Shadow Financial Regulatory Committee, a private group of recognized experts on U.S. financial institutions:

> . . . that the Credit Reform Act of 1990 be amended to require the Office of Management and Budget (OMB) and the Congressional Budget Office (CBO) to measure the annual cost of the credit enhancements that each GSE enjoys. This annual cost should be included in the federal budget and a reserve fund should be established sufficient to absorb the losses that might occur. This is a prerequisite to rationally evaluating the justification for continuing these enterprises.[12]

The committee went on to say that the GSEs' opportunity to borrow from the Treasury and their inferred government guarantees "explain why interest rates on GSE debt average at least 100 basis points below rates paid by private borrowers with similar balance sheets." (One basis point is one hundredth of 1 percent.) On GSE liabilities of $1.7 trillion, a 1 percent subsidy would amount to $17 billion a year.

OMB and CBO should be able to agree on reasonable estimates of the various GSE interest rate subsidies, which may well be 100 basis points or more for certain maturities or types of some GSE issues but much less for others, based on congressional and administration staff studies that were near completion at the time this book went to press.

A distinction must be made between two subsidy measures: the cost to the government and the benefit to the subsidized borrower. A GSE might benefit from government backing by saving 100 basis points in its borrowing costs, but the cost to government might be estimated to be as low as, say, 35 points, based on estimates that the competition from government-backed GSE borrowings raises Treasury borrowing costs by 10 basis points and that a 25 basis point charge would provide an adequate reserve for losses. Thus a 35 basis point guarantee fee might cover the government costs, but it would leave the GSE with a 65 basis point subsidy advantage over competing private institutions. (Under the Federal Credit Reform Act of 1990, subsidies on direct and guaranteed loans are measured by the estimated costs to government, rather than the benefit to borrower, but these subsidy measures are not for the purpose of establishing fees to be charged borrowers.)

The Shadow Financial Regulatory Committee's recommendation provides for much needed recognition of the GSE subsidies as costs to the federal budget. These costs, however, should be borne by the GSEs rather than the federal taxpayer.

A transition period of several years may be necessary to phase in guarantee or user fees that cover the full value of the various federal credit enhancements enjoyed by each GSE. (Some GSEs have more tax advantages, more preferential treatment of their securities, and greater recourse to Treasury financial assistance than others, and the GSEs vary in the strength of their balance sheets and their acceptance in the securities markets.) GSE stockholder rights would need to be recognized, and in some cases initial fees might apply only to new liabilities rather than to outstanding debt. An initial fee of, say, 25 basis points on some appropriate measure of liabilities for each GSE would seem reasonable. A gradual fee increase over the years would give the GSEs time to adjust and to consider giving up the federal credit enhancements rather than pay the escalating fees. Some GSEs may never sever all ties to the government, but at least they would be established on a more competitive basis in the market and at less cost to the taxpayers.

There should be no question about the fee-paying ability of the major GSEs, Fannie Mae and Freddie Mac, which generally account for about 85 percent of the total outstanding GSE liabilities. Consider the following statement by Standard & Poor's:

> Freddie's advantage is that it can finance purchases of mortgages at quasi-agency rates. The company also generates impressive returns: return on equity [ROE] was over 20% in 1995. The excellent ROE can be partially explained by . . . highly efficient operation and the fact that it competes in essentially a two-company market.[13]

The other participant in the two-company market, what economists call a duopoly, is of course Fannie Mae. In each of the past ten years the ROE has exceeded 20 percent for Freddie Mac and 25 percent for Fannie Mae. A 1991 investment of $10,000 was worth in 1996, $54,615 in the case of Freddie Mac stock and $39,255 in the case of Fannie Mae stock.[14] Surely, both agencies can easily afford to pay, starting now, at least a nominal fee to cover a portion of their substantial costs to the American taxpayer. The purpose of these agencies was to increase the availability of housing credit, not subsidize the price, not enrich stockholders, nor increase the federal budget deficit.

Would such fees or removal of the GSE subsidies increase the cost of housing? Yes. Without the implied U.S. Treasury backing of their securities, the GSEs would have to pay higher interest rates on their borrowings, and that added cost would be passed on primarily to the homeowner, as would any fee. Why abolish such a democratic subsidy that benefits virtually everybody? That's why. If the benefit of a subsidy to private activities goes to virtually everybody and an equal cost is borne by virtually everybody (as taxpayers), the net benefit to virtually everybody is zero. Indeed, because of the present lack of competition and the administrative costs of the GSEs, there may well be a significant net cost to virtually everybody.

CONCLUSION

The dramatically increased role of federal and federally assisted borrowing in our economy raises serious questions about the viability of private credit markets. We have reached a point where most of the credit market instruments available to private investors are securities issued or guaranteed by federal government instrumentalities. As more and more credit risks are shifted from private lenders to government guarantors, the quality of credit and the economic allocation of credit surely suffer. Government-sponsored enterprises are the fastest growing federal credit aids. Unlike federal direct and guaranteed loans, the GSEs are not now subject to federal budgetary constraints. The government subsidies to the GSEs also insulate them from competition in the private market. After decades of government subsidies, it is time that the highly profitable GSEs began to pay fees to offset their costs to the government and to reduce their unfair advantage in the market.

8 The National Debt and Social Security

T HIS BOOK would not be complete if I did not deal with a relatively new myth that raises concerns about the impact of the national debt on the financial health of Social Security. As used here, the term *Social Security* refers to the Old-Age and Survivors Insurance and Disability (OASDI) Trust Funds, which finance the traditional Social Security system. We are not discussing Medicare Part A (hospital insurance) or Medicare Part B (supplemental medical insurance), which are financed from separate funds and must be considered in the broader context of overall health care reform.

THE SOCIAL SECURITY PROBLEM

The problem with the Social Security trust fund is that it is expected to run out of money in the year 2030. That is the best estimate of the Social Security Board of Trustees. It could be much sooner or later. The date 2030 is the intermediate estimate in a range of estimates provided by the trustees in their 1995 annual report.[1]

Figure 8-1 shows the estimated balances in the Social Security fund from 1995 to 2030. The fund balance increases rapidly from $.5 trillion in 1995 to $3.3 trillion in 2020. Then, as the baby boomers retire in large numbers (baby boomers being defined here as they are in the trustees' report—those persons born "from the end of World War II through the mid-1960s"[2]), the fund balance declines sharply to $2.3 trillion in 2025 and to $0 in 2030.

Figure 8-1 Estimated Social Security fund balances, calendar years 1995–2030 (trillions of dollars)

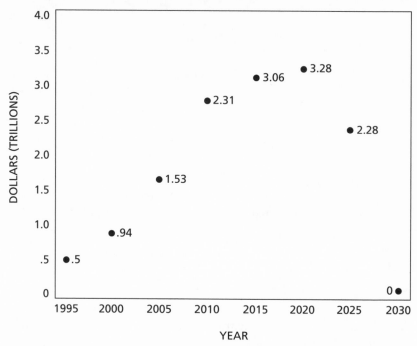

YEAR

Source: 1995 Annual Report of the Board of Trustees of the Federal Old-Age and Survivors Insurance and Disability Insurance Trust Funds, House Document 104-57 (Washington, D.C.: GPO, 1995), 181.

The trustees would, I think, agree that their underlying assumptions as to the course of the economy, inflation, interest rates, and demographic and other critical variables over the next thirty-five years are iffy. Yet it seems likely that some significant changes in Social Security will need to be made to ensure that adequate benefits will be available for the retiring baby boomers.

As the baby boomers retire, the number of workers covered by Social Security (and thus paying into the trust funds) will shrink dramatically relative to the number of retired people receiving Social Security benefits. As stated in the trustees' report: "In 1994, there were about 3.3 workers for every beneficiary. As indicated, this ratio is expected to decline substantially in the future. . . . Most of this decline will occur as the relatively large number of persons born during the 'baby boom' . . . reaches retirement age and begins to receive benefits. At the same time, the relatively small number of persons born during the subsequent period of low fertility rates will comprise the labor force."[3]

The report then shows a chart that projects a sharp decline in the number of workers per beneficiary from 3.3 in 1994 to about 2.0 in 2030 (and then a more gradual decline to 1.8 in 2070). Put another way, the burden that retirees place on workers would increase by 67 percent.[4] At the same time, those workers will need to cope with the rising costs of educating their children to meet the technical demands of an increasingly complex world.

REASONABLE LONG-TERM SOLUTIONS

The trustees' best estimate is that the shortfall, or "actuarial deficit," in Social Security trust funds over the next seventy-five years will be 2.17 percent of the payroll tax base. That means that the long-term financing problem could be solved by instituting an immediate increase of 1.09 percentage points in the Social Security taxes paid by both employers and employees; the current tax on each would increase from 6.2 percent to 7.3 percent.[5] Of course, the longer the increase in the Social Security tax is delayed, the greater it will have to be.

Alternatively, Social Security tax increases might be minimized or postponed by some modest reductions in benefits. For example, the retirement age, which is now sixty-five but is scheduled to go up gradually to sixty-seven by 2027, might be raised sooner and/or set at an older age. When the retirement age was set at sixty-five in the original Social Security legislation in 1935, life expectancy for newborn Americans was about sixty. So more than half of the working population was expected to die before receiving Social Security benefits. The benefits flowed initially to the lucky people who beat the odds in the mortality tables. Life expectancy has since increased to about seventy-six, but Congress has been unwilling to take the politically unpopular step of putting the Social Security retirement age more in line with life expectancy.

Over the sixty-year life of Social Security, we have moved from a system in which the average person was expected to die before collecting a nickel to a system in which the average person should expect to collect benefits for more than a decade. I say "should" because current opinion surveys show that most young people do not expect Social Security to be there for them when they retire.

Consider the following *Wall Street Journal* report of a 1995 survey of American attitudes toward retirement security: "Both twentysome-things and boomers are highly skeptical that the government will fund their retirement. A vast majority of both generations—more than 80% of twentysomethings and more than 70% of boomers—believe Social Security won't be available to support their retirement."[6] They are wrong. They fail to recognize the ever-growing political power of Social Security recipients and the fact that, as indicated above (and below), it should be relatively easy to fix the Social Security financing problem if action is taken in the near future.

Various combinations of reforms have been suggested by Social Security experts to reduce the actuarial deficit in the Social Security fund. Former Social Security Commissioner Robert M. Ball, a member of the Advisory Council on Social Security, made a proposal to the council in 1996, which included this statement:

> The proposals I back greatly reduce the deficit immediately—from 2.17 percent of payroll to 0.80 [percent]—and do not increase Social Security deductions from wages or the matching contributions of employers. They reduce benefits only an average of 3 percent below present law.
>
> The proposed changes are: 1. The extension of coverage to those 3.7 million state and local employees who are still excluded from the Social Security program (most are covered). 2. An increase in the period over which benefits are computed from 35 years to 38 years. 3. A change in the policy governing the taxation of Social Security benefits so that the income tax is applied individually to benefits in excess of what the worker paid in, as is now true for other contributory defined benefit plans. As in present law, the proceeds of the tax would be

deposited in the Social Security trust fund. Also, when Medicare is refinanced, at least by 2010 to 2020 when the baby boom generation is retiring, the part of the tax on Social Security benefits now going to Hospital Insurance should be redirected to Social Security. (Many members of the Council do not agree on this last point, although there is a majority for the rest of the three legislative programs.) When these changes are added to the correction in the upward bias in the CPI as announced in March 1996 by the Bureau of Labor Statistics (CPI − 0.21), the deficit of 2.17 is reduced to 0.80, and the date of Trust Fund exhaustion moves from 2030 under present law to 2050.[7]

Mr. Ball then proposes that the remaining deficit of .80 of payroll be eliminated by investing up to 40 percent of the Social Security fund in a broad stock index fund, such as the Russell 3000 or Wilshire 5000. Such investments would be managed by private fund managers selected by an independent board established along the lines of the Federal Retirement Thrift Investment Board (discussed later in this chapter). Mr. Ball suggests that the 40 percent goal be reached gradually over the period 2000 through 2015, which would reduce the 75-year Social Security fund deficit by about .90 percent of payroll. So long as proposals such as Mr. Ball's are adopted in the near future, there should be no need for drastic actions when the baby boomers retire.

Why, then, all the fuss? Why do young people believe that Social Security will not be there for them when they reach retirement age?

WHAT'S *NOT* TRUE ABOUT SOCIAL SECURITY

The leaders of both political parties have been grossly misleading on the nature of the Social Security financing problem—the Democrats by claiming that proposals to balance the budget would result in "looting" the Social Security trust funds,[8] and the Republicans by claiming that balancing the budget would solve the Social Security financing problem.[9] Both parties are on the one hand unduly alarmist about the Social Security financing problem and on the other hand unwilling to make the politically unpopular decisions needed to deal with the problem before it actually does become alarming. House Speaker Newt Gingrich put it this way:

> The money the government supposedly has been putting aside from the baby boomers' Social Security taxes *is not there.* The government has been borrowing that money to pay for the budget deficit. So when the baby boomers get set to retire, where's the money to pay them going to come from? Well, can't the government just borrow more money? The honest answer is no. No system, no country, is wealthy enough to have unlimited borrowing.
>
> But the answer is clear. The key to protecting the baby baby boomers' Social Security is to balance the budget. That way, by the time the baby boomers retire, the government will be financially sound enough to pay them. The problem is not Social Security. After all, Social Security would be fine if the federal government would stop borrowing the money. The government can stop borrowing the money when we balance the budget. It is just that simple."[10]

That's nonsense. (Any time a politician, be it Ross Perot or Newt Gingrich, says that the solution to a large and continuing national problem is "just that simple," you have a pretty good indicator that he is either uninformed or not yet prepared to deal with the problem.)

Speaker Gingrich is wrong on all three counts. The money that the government has been putting aside in the Social Security trust funds *is* there, fully invested in the safest interest-bearing securities in the world. The problem *is* Social Security, not the budget deficit. Social Security would *not* be fine if the federal government stopped borrowing the money; it would be a lot worse off because it would be losing the interest it now earns on its investments in U.S. Treasury securities.

The fact that the money that goes into the trust fund is invested in Treasury securities and then spent by the government does not mean that the trust fund has been looted. Other trust funds, private as well as public, invest in Treasury or other securities issued by borrowers who spend the borrowed money.[11] Why else would they borrow? A real shocker would be a trust fund with money that is *not* invested and thus not producing earnings for the beneficiaries of the trust.

Also, the fact that the government is running large current budget deficits is not in itself a threat to the earnings or safety of the Social Security trust fund. If the government were to run a budget surplus, instead of a deficit, the Social Security trust fund surplus (which would be invested in Treasury securities) would automatically reduce Treasury's outstanding debt in the market, and the trust fund itself would be in the same position as it would be with a federal budget deficit.

A BIG FIRST STEP

Despite the overwhelming clarity of the arguments for making minor adjustments in Social Security soon, politicians aren't likely to make changes to the much feared "third rail of American politics" ("touch it and you're dead") in the near future. Because of this political timidity about changing Social Security taxes or benefits, the compelling need now is for prompt reconsideration of the investment policies of the trust fund. The shift from traditional pay-as-you-go financing to a policy of building up large surpluses, instituted in 1983 (in anticipation of the retirement needs of the baby boomers), has made investment earnings a much more important factor in the growth of the fund. Also, the development of stock index funds in recent years has provided an acceptable vehicle for the investment of public funds in private equity securities, which have produced substantially higher long-term earnings than the Treasury securities in which the fund is now invested.

The federal government is unique in its policy of investing its major trust funds only in its own securities.[12] There are approximately 800,000 private (insured and noninsured) and state and local government pension funds in this country. For the last thirty years more than one-third of the assets in these funds has been invested in the stock market, while about half of the assets in private noninsured funds has been put in stocks.[13]

The only feasible way to increase the Social Security fund's earnings significantly is to invest a substantial portion of it in the stock market. Over the past thirty years, the average annual return of the stocks in the Standard & Poor's 500 index was approximately 11 percent, compared with a return of about 8 percent from the Treasury securities in which the Social Security trust fund is invested. A reasonable assumption would be that the 3 percentage-point spread in favor of stocks will be maintained for the foreseeable future.

Investment of one-half of the Social Security fund in stocks would solve more than half of the long-run Social Security financing problem (based on former Social Security Commissioner Ball's above calculation that investment of 40 percent of the fund in stocks would solve .90 percentage points of the 2.17 percent of payroll deficit over the next 75 years). Such an investment could be authorized in separate legislation, or it could be the major component of a package of reforms that might include some modest Social Security tax increases, a delayed retirement age, and/or benefit reductions.

It might be argued that any projected increase in the earnings of the Social Security trust fund might have the perverse effect of further delaying action on the reforms that are politically unpopular. Nonetheless, it's likely that the promise of increased investment earnings will attract at least some additional support for a legislative package that includes the less palatable measures.

As a U.S. Treasury Department economist and public debt manager, I was frequently asked to respond to proposals to invest the Social Security or other government funds in the stock market. We opposed such proposals for the following reasons: (1) government ownership and control of private corporations (a.k.a. socialism) are incompatible with our free-enterprise economy and would raise serious conflicts of interest for public officials, and (2) stocks are too risky an investment for public funds. Treasury Department testimony before Congress in 1988 contained the following statement on the specific question of investing the Social Security trust funds in the stock market: "Aggressive movement of the funds into equities and other private securities would entail higher risk of loss or default than Treasury obligations, a risk unsuitable to the social policy goal of the programs. If ownership of equities or private sector bonds were contemplated, significant problems would arise as to potential federal control of corporations, the allocation of investment resources, and the conduct of business. We recommend against such involvement."[14]

These problems can now be avoided by investing in broad stock index funds so that the government's interest in any particular corporation in the index is relatively small and indirect. Prohibiting the government from voting the stock avoids the problem of government control. While individual stocks or sectors of the economy may well be unacceptable risks for government funds, a broad stock index fund provides the relative safety of diversification. Although the stock market is volatile in the short run, the experience of the past fifty years shows that this volatility is not a serious risk for long-term investments, such as retirement funds.

Accordingly, in 1986 the Congress authorized stock index fund investments (without voting rights) by the Federal Retirement Thrift Investment Board, which administers the Thrift Savings Plan for federal employees. As the first executive director of the board (1986–1994), I encountered no significant problems as we selected an index (the S&P 500), obtained competitive bids from large index fund managers, and established a highly efficient stock fund with minimal administrative expenses. By 1996, 1 million federal employees had elected to invest $13 billion in the board's stock index fund. I see no reason why the Social Security trust fund should not have the same stock investment advantage as the Thrift Savings Plan.

THE PRIVATIZATION OPTION

The hot-button Social Security issue of 1996 is "privatization." It is the darling of many conservative groups and the private investment community. As stated in the *Wall Street Journal:*

It could be the biggest bonanza in the history of the mutual-fund industry.

The lure: a pot of money worth trillions of dollars.

The target: Social Security. The goal: to revise the program so individual workers could shunt the payroll taxes they pay into IRA-like savings accounts that would allow lump-sum withdrawals at retirement.[15]

A variety of schemes have been proposed, but the common theme is to permit individuals to manage the investment of a portion of their Social Security contribution in an IRA. For example, instead of the current system of deducting 6.2 percent from an employee's pay and depositing all of it in the Social Security trust fund, the employee would be permitted to allocate, say, 2 percent of pay to a savings deposit, a mutual fund, or another IRA-type investment vehicle. (This assumes that there would be no change from the tax treatment of Social Security contributions; employee allocations would be on an after-tax basis, but their earnings would be tax-deferred.) If the employee chose to do that, the deposit in the Social Security trust fund would be reduced to 4.2 percent of pay and the employee's Social Security benefits would be reduced proportionately to avoid a cost to the fund. Would Social Security recipients be better off under such a privatization scheme? Probably not.

A major problem with the privatization option is that it would most likely result in a significant reduction in total retirement income, especially for low- to moderate-income employees. Even if politicians could resist demands for early withdrawals from the privatized accounts to meet medical, educational, or other hardship needs, it is unlikely that the investments in the privatized accounts would outperform the investments in the Social Security fund. In calculating the reduction in Social Security benefits for employees who chose the 2 percent privatization option, the government presumably would calculate how much more the Social Security fund would have grown had it not lost that payroll contribution. The interest rate used in the calculation would be the rate on the special Treasury obligations in which the Social Security fund is invested. That rate is generally higher than the rate paid to other investors in Treasury obligations of similar maturities.[16] (Over the past thirty years the Social Security trust fund rate has averaged about 8 percent a year.) Consequently, for employees to do as well on their private investments as they would have done in the Social Security fund, they would generally need to beat the rate on Treasury long-term marketable securities. Yet that long-term Treasury rate is generally much higher than the rates offered on government-insured deposits by banks, savings and loan associations, and credit unions, as well as on other relatively safe IRA-type investments that are popular among low- and moderate-income savers.

The privatization option would probably not be advantageous unless a substantial portion of the private investment were in the stock market. But low- and moderate-income individuals are generally too risk averse to invest heavily in stocks. For example, a 1992 survey of consumer finances by the University of Michigan found that 9 percent of families with incomes from $10,000 to $25,000, 18 percent of families with incomes from $25,000 to $50,000, 31 percent of families with incomes from $50,000 to $100,000, and 49 percent of families with incomes over $100,000 invested directly in stocks. The survey showed similar patterns for the percentage of families investing in mutual funds and retirement accounts, both of which include some stock funds.[17] (Even if participants were to put their entire 2 percent contribution into stocks, that amount would account for only 16 percent of the total 12.4 percent employer/employee Social Security contributions, compared with the possible 50 percent stock investment I suggested earlier.) Also, financial advisory fees, investment management fees, and other administrative costs associated with private stock investments could significantly reduce the net benefits to low-income savers with relatively small accounts.

High-income employees would be better able to bear the transaction costs associated with private investments and would probably be more attracted to the privatization option. However, if the Social Security fund lost large amounts of contributions from high-income workers, such adverse selection could weaken the fund to the point that either Social Security taxes would go up or benefits to lower income workers would go down.

Another defect in the privatization option is that it would foolishly shift investment risk from the group (all Social Security participants) to the individual. This violates the fundamental insurance principle of shifting risk from the individual to the group; risk is more easily borne if it is widely distributed. Also, since Social Security is a social insurance system in which the government guarantees a level of benefits, and these benefits can be provided at a lower cost if the investment risk is retained by the fund rather than shifted to the individual. The implicit self-insurance premium would be higher for the individuals than for the fund.

Over the long run, many individuals who elected the privatization option would realize that their total retirement income was smaller than that of their relatives and friends who remained in the current Social Security system. By then it would be too late. The investment losses would be irretrievable, as would the fees paid to private investment advisors and managers.

The privatization option confuses the roles of *defined benefit* and *defined contribution* retirement plans. Traditional retirement plans in the United States are defined benefit plans. Common practice has been for an employer to make periodic contributions to an employee retirement fund that, when invested, are expected to provide a predetermined level of benefits. If the fund investments underperform, the employer must increase its contributions to provide the guaranteed benefits. If the fund overperforms, the employer may reduce its contributions. The employer makes the investment decisions and takes the investment risk, so the employees neither gain from investment overperformance nor lose from underperformance. The employer has a strong self-interest in seeking the best professional fund management.

The newer and faster-growing retirement funds are defined contribution plans, such as the Thrift Savings Plan for federal employees. These plans are generally referred to as 401(k) plans (named after the relevant section of the Internal Revenue Code) and are now standard offerings by large U.S. corporations as supplements to traditional employer-sponsored defined benefit plans. As the name suggests, the contributions, not the benefits, are defined. Generally, these contributions are made by voluntary deductions from the employees' pretax salary and partial matching contributions from the employer.

For example, the federal Thrift Savings Plan provides for employee contributions up to 10 percent of the employee's pay and employer contributions up to 5 percent of pay.

The employer provides for professional management of defined contribution funds, but the employee is permitted to choose from a variety of stock, bond, or other investment options. Unlike defined benefit plans, each employee has a separate account and bears the investment risk. Corporations generally welcome this opportunity to shift the investment risk to the employees, and employees welcome having greater control of this portion of their retirement savings. The employer generally absorbs much of the plan's administrative costs and provides investment information and retirement counseling at no cost to the employees.

The Social Security retirement system is a unique defined benefit plan in that the fund is financed by payroll taxes of both employers and employees. The fund is conservatively invested in Treasury securities. As investments have not grown fast enough to cover rapidly growing guaranteed benefit payments to retirees, payroll taxes have been increased. Social Security is similar to other defined benefit plans in that benefits are not dependent upon investment performance and individual employees have no control over investments. Yet the investment risk is in effect borne by future Social Security taxpayers as a group.

Since politicians are now afraid to take the political risk of either cutting Social Security benefits or raising Social Security taxes, there seems to be growing sentiment in Washington for a structural change that would reduce the benefit to tax ratio without appearing to do so. The privatization option would do just that.

Polls show that the privatization option is very popular.[18] People apparently are so pessimistic about their future Social Security benefits that they would leap at the opportunity to control the investment of a portion of their Social Security taxes. Political leaders have been irresponsible in misleading young people to believe that Social Security benefits will be substantially reduced by the time they retire. The government would have a moral, if not legal, responsibility to inform people fully about the investment implications of privatization. While this information should deter people from electing the option, many people are already so apprehensive about Social Security and mistrustful of the government that they might well seize the option anyway.

THE PERSONAL INVESTMENT FUND OPTION

An alternative approach proposed by Senators Robert Kerrey (D-Neb.) and Alan Simpson (R-Wyo.), is to offer the 2 percent privatization option outlined above along with another option that would permit employees to contribute to a 401(k)-type fund like the federal Thrift Savings Fund. The two senators introduced legislation (S. 824) in 1995 that would establish (1) in the Social Security Administration (SSA) a Personal Investment Fund Board "in the same manner as the Federal Retirement Thrift Investment Board" and (2) in the Treasury Department a Personal Investment Fund (PIF) "in the same manner as the Thrift Savings Fund."

The PIF option would have the potential for certain economies of scale in the consolidation of recordkeeping, investment management, communication, and other administrative functions. Yet there would remain the perhaps fatal problem of shifting investment risk from the group to risk-averse individuals who probably would not invest enough in the stock market to realize more retirement income than if they had remained in the Social Security system.

Moreover, S. 824 would need to be revised to make the PIF board an independent agency. The PIF board could not operate in the same manner as the Thrift Investment Board if the board were a part of the Social Security Administration and the PIF were part of the Treasury Department. The Thrift Investment Board was established as a separate agency, independent of the administration, with a fiduciary responsibility to act solely in the interest of the participants and beneficiaries of the Thrift Savings Plan. That responsibility could not be properly discharged by a board subject to the direction of other agencies with different, and inevitably conflicting, interests. When such conflicts arise among administration agencies they are generally resolved by the Justice Department or the White House, both of which are expected to act in the interest of the United States, the administration, and the president, rather than the narrower special interests of a particular program such as the Thrift Savings Plan. Thus the Kerrey-Simpson bill would need to be modified to structure the PIF as a wholly independent agency to act solely in the interest of the people who elected to contribute to the fund.

Finally, the administration of any plan as large as the PIF would be a daunting task. With over 2 million participants, the Thrift Savings Plan is the largest defined contribution plan in the country and an enormous administrative challenge. Social Security, with more than 120 million covered employees, is administratively dependent on many millions of employers, including the self-employed, the mom and pop stores, and the households employing part-time maids and nannies earning as little as $1,000 a year—not a seamless operation. If possible at all, it is highly unlikely PIF could ever meet the high fiduciary standards expected of pension plan administrators today.

The most effective, and perhaps only feasible, way to ensure that Social Security participants are given the stock investment benefits available to virtually all other large retirement plans in the country is to permit the Treasury to invest a large portion, not to exceed 50 percent, of the Social Security trust fund in a broad stock index fund, such as a S&P 500 or a Wilshire 5000 fund. The investment risk would remain with the group, rather than shift to the individual. There would be no need for expensive individual account maintenance or employee communications programs. The administrative costs would be negligible. The entire operation could be managed by a dozen Treasury staff or by a small independent agency to avoid any conflict of interests, compared with a staff perhaps a hundred times larger to administer the PIF or perhaps a thousand times larger to administer the privatization option (including staff of private institutions). This proposal would go a long way toward resolving the long-term Social Security financing problems.

THE GREATEST INVESTMENT: TODAY'S CHILDREN

The Social Security financing problem, while significant, is very manageable as long as some modest action on taxes, benefits, and/or investments is taken in the near future. Moreover, we should not allow the financing problem, or its resolution, to obscure the underlying economics of the care and feeding of the baby boomers.

First, the baby boom is by definition a temporary problem. The boom was followed by the so-called baby bust, which will be reflected in a reduced number of new retirees after 2030.

Second, since our economy prospered during the postwar period of the baby boom, we should be able to deal with the economics of retiring this group. Indeed, it probably cost society more to feed, clothe, and educate the baby boomers in their first two decades of life than it will to care for the greatly diminished number of boomers who will live long enough to enjoy a prolonged retirement. While medical care costs are much higher for the elderly, as a father of three baby boomers I recall that obstetric, pediatric, and orthodontic care was not cheap. As stated by Robert Ball and Henry Aaron, director of Economic Studies at the Brookings Institution,

> The true measure of the burden of the dependent population is the ratio of the dependent, old and young, to active workers. . . . As the following numbers indicate, the dependency burden will never be as high as it was in 1960, when the baby boomers were children:

Year	Dependency Population Per 1,000 Active Workers
1960	904
1993	707
2010	656
2040	789
2070	826

> As economist Frank Ackerman quipped: "If we could afford to live through the childhood of the baby boom generation, we can afford to live through their retirement."[19]

Third, rather than say, as Mr. Gingrich did, "The key to protecting the baby boomers' Social Security is to balance the budget," we should recognize that the real key to protecting the baby boomers' Social Security is to provide now for the health, education, and welfare of the children of the baby boomers. That is our greatest investment in the future.

Today, the baby boomers are in their early thirties to early fifties, the prime of their working lives, and are the principal means of support of both today's children and today's elderly. Likewise, when the baby boomers retire, their children will be their principal means of support. The quality of that support will depend on the productivity of their children, which in turn will depend on our investment in those children today.

All baby boomers, whether they have children of their own or not, should know that they must invest in today's children to ensure their own personal financial security in retirement. It is not enough for boomers to increase their personal savings or to invest in the technology and physical facilities needed to enhance the productivity of tomorrow's workers. An educated workforce will be essential to achieve the required level of productivity.

Yet we often hear outraged complaints from childless adults that their tax money is being used to educate "other people's children." They do not seem to understand that their own future livelihood is totally dependent on "other people's children." Such complaints are no more ironic than those of a small minority of twentysomethings who, having just accepted some $200,000 worth of education from their parents' generation, charge that generation with selfishness for having run up a large national debt, even though the younger generation will inherit both the assets and liabilities represented by the debt.

Significant productivity increases will be necessary as a diminished labor force is called on to support an expanded group of retirees. Without such increased production per worker, a shortage of goods will lead to price increases, and it is likely that the baby boomers will suffer a significant decline in the purchasing power of their retirement dollars. Inflation could soon decimate their retirement savings. That's the economic reality; if you're not working, you're dependent on the productivity of those who are.

Consider, for example, an average Joe retiring at sixty-five, who would normally be expected to live for about another fifteen years. Typically Joe might look forward to meeting the necessities and conveniences of life from Social Security and from a pension from his former employer. Beyond that, the money for the new car, travel, vacations, and other luxuries might have to come from personal savings.

Let's say that Joe's life savings total $200,000 and that he wants to preserve that purchasing power over the next fifteen years as a nest egg for medical or other emergencies, possibly nursing-home care, or for his estate for the benefit of, say, his grandchildren's education or a favorite charity. So Joe wants his nest egg to grow with the rate of inflation. How much current income can Joe expect from his nest egg in order to enjoy his "golden years"? Suppose Joe invests his $200,000 over the next fifteen years at an average annual return of 9 percent, which might appear to be a pretty good return, since the average annual rate on long-term Treasury securities over the last thirty years was only about 8 percent. Assume that Joe lives in New York and that perhaps 40 percent of those earnings go to federal, state, and local income taxes. That would leave a nominal return of 5.4 percent, which happens to have been just about the average annual rate of inflation over the last thirty years. Thus the net return after taxes and inflation might well be zero. So Joe would receive no real income from his investment over the fifteen-year period and would just barely preserve the purchasing power of his original $200,000 principal. That is, his nest egg would grow in inflated dollars to about $440,000, but it would be worth just $200,000 in today's dollars. Put another way, with annual inflation of 5.4 percent, a house that cost $200,000 today would cost $440,000 fifteen years from now.

Worse yet, most retirees probably would not earn an investment return as high as the 9 percent in the above example, because they prefer "safer" investments such as short-term Treasury bills and notes, bank certificates of deposit, money market funds, or other debt instruments that had average returns substantially below 9 percent over the last thirty years. Thus, at the end of fifteen years, not only would

these retirees receive no real net earnings from their financial investments, but they would actually suffer a loss in the purchasing power
of their principal.

One of my first jobs as a young economist in the Treasury Department in the 1950s was drafting responses to irate citizens who wrote
to the secretary of the Treasury or the president. They complained
that their life's savings were being eroded because they invested in
long-term Treasury bonds, which they had thought would provide
them with a comfortable nest egg in retirement.

For example, consider the 3¼ percent thirty-year bonds issued
by Secretary George Humphrey in 1953. As noted in chapter 4, Humphrey was strongly criticized in Congress for paying such a high rate
of interest on long-term bonds. Many investors saw this bond issue
as an excellent long-term retirement investment guaranteed by the
full faith and credit of the U.S. government, especially since they had
been accustomed to getting much less (interest rates on Treasury
securities had been capped at 2½ percent during World War II).
Moreover, inflation was virtually nonexistent in the early 1950s, as
it had been in the prewar years. Humphrey's bonds had to be a sure
thing. As it turned out, the congressional critics were wrong: the
Treasury made out handsomely on the 3¼ percent bonds (when the
bonds reached maturity in 1983 Treasury refunded them with new
thirty-year bonds at what was then the going rate of 12 percent), and
the investors had taken quite a beating. The after-tax return on the
3¼ percent bonds was quickly lost to inflation in the 1960s. By 1970,
with inflation at 5.7 percent and interest yields on long-term Treasury
bonds above 7 percent, the 3¼ percent bonds were selling in the
secondary market for just 62 cents on the dollar.[20] So, a little more
than halfway through the life of the bonds, net earnings (after inflation) were negative and investors had paper losses of 38 percent of
their original investment. Can it happen again? Sure. Treasury sold
thirty-year bonds at rates below 6 percent in 1993, and it does not
take much imagination to envision another inflationary period with
long-term interest rates returning to the 14 percent levels of 1981.

Even in Treasury securities, the safest investments in the world,
inflation can quickly wipe out a substantial portion of the purchasing

power of tomorrow's retirement savings. The best protection against this kind of loss is to provide the kind of education for children today that will maximize their productivity as members of tomorrow's labor force and thus minimize inflationary pressures.

CONCLUSION

The Social Security financing problem has nothing to do with the federal deficit or debt. The Social Security trust fund is expected to run out of money in 2030 largely because of the costs of paying benefits to retired baby boomers and the failure to increase the minimum retirement age as life expectancy has increased over the last sixty years. The number of workers paying into the Social Security fund relative to the number of retirees receiving benefits is expected to decline from 3.3 in 1994 to about 2.0 in 2030. Yet the actuarial deficit in the Social Security fund over the next seventy-five years can probably be eliminated if we make relatively painless adjustments (a change in the way the fund is invested, modest increases in the payroll tax and minimum retirement age, and so forth) *now*.

The claims by leaders in both political parties (1) that a balanced federal budget will cure the Social Security financing problem and (2) that current budget deficits are being financed by "looting" the Social Security trust fund are pure political nonsense. The fund is fully invested in the safest securities in the world. There is no likelihood of default, economically or politically. The problem is that not enough money is being put into the fund because neither political party has had the courage to start making the adjustments that will prevent a serious financial crisis for the next generation.

Whatever is done with the Social Security fund, there is no way to avoid the underlying economic reality that the baby boomers and other retirees will enjoy a comfortable retirement only if the productivity of the workers at the time permits it. That future productivity depends on how well we tend to the health, education, and welfare of today's children.

If the workers of tomorrow do not have the education or skills to increase productivity to the extent needed to support a growing number of elderly people, the inevitable inflation may cut so deeply into the purchasing power of the elderly population that its members will find their life's savings quickly diminished. The somber thought of the seventeenth-century writer John Donne—"never send to know for whom the bell tolls; It tolls for *thee*"—might well apply to the school bell. We are all in this together.

9   Why the Myths Persist

W HY DO THE MYTHS about the public debt persist? Why do highly intelligent and experienced politicians and business executives seem to embrace these myths as articles of faith? There are many explanations.

POTOMAC FEVER

Perhaps part of the reason why some top Washington officials have difficulty in communicating common sense to the American people is that they are afflicted with a form of Potomac fever—a malady generally thought of as an addiction to the heady business of formulating national policy and securing a place in history. But Potomac fever can take many virulent forms. One common form springs from the preconception of many top business executives that a stay in Washington is like an adventure in (Alice's) Wonderland. When successful executives receive "the call" to come to Washington to serve in the president's cabinet, they sometimes expect to find there an absence of reason, which becomes a self-fulfilling expectation when they leave their own reason behind in the process.

One example of this phenomenon that comes to mind has to do with a secretary of the Treasury appointed some years ago. He had been a top banking executive, which was true of several Treasury secretaries I served, and thus when he came to Washington he was confident in his understanding of the world of finance and Treasury debt. Just a few days after he was appointed, the secretary was called on to appear before Congress to explain the need for an immediate increase in the statutory public debt ceiling, a law that limits the amount of money the Treasury may borrow to meet the needs of the government.

My colleagues and I in the Treasury had drafted some standard testimony for the secretary. The draft testimony was very much like that given each year by his immediate predecessors. It indicated simply that if Congress did not increase the public debt ceiling promptly, the Treasury would run out of money and be unable to pay the bills for the programs enacted by Congress. Earlier Treasury secretaries had tried to downplay the debt-ceiling legislation as a routine administrative matter. Congress had no choice but to authorize the additional borrowing. They had already appropriated funds for the additional spending that made the additional borrowing necessary—no point in closing the barn door after the horse gets away.

When we met with the secretary to answer questions he might have about the draft, we found that he had made a change. He had added a sentence that read, "As Benjamin Franklin said, 'Neither a borrower nor a lender be.' " (It was actually William Shakespeare, not Franklin, who said that.[1]) We advised the secretary not to use that quote. Given the fact that our economy cannot function without credit, such a statement would hardly have enhanced public confidence in the new administration. So the sentence was deleted, and the administration was spared a headline in the next day's newspaper that might have read, "President's new banker says no more borrowing."

I relate this story not to poke fun at this unnamed cabinet member but to illustrate the strange effect that the crossing of the Potomac river has on some new government appointees' common sense. It is not likely that the secretary would have so decried borrowing when he was on Wall Street, but somehow it seemed to him appropriate to do so in the Washington Wonderland.

This is not to suggest that common sense should always be the test for getting by in Washington. Indeed, as indicated above, common sense would seem to dictate that Washington officials explain to the people that the national debt, because we owe it largely to ourselves, cannot be likened to the burdensome debts of others, such as individuals, corporations, or state and local governments.

Yet when I was in the Treasury we would not advise the incumbent secretary to say in public that the burden of the national debt was lighter because we owed it to ourselves. We had learned from bitter experience that it would be counterproductive. The media would have a ball; and the Senate Finance Committee, which had jurisdiction over the debt limit legislation, would explode with righteous indignation, as each political party sought to outdo the other in apparent fiscal rectitude. Nor would the private financial markets regard such a statement from the Secretary of the Treasury as a confidence builder.

THE CORPORATE STATESMAN

Much of the public confusion about the national debt arises from misinformation from influential business leaders. This is especially true of the top corporate executives who, having proven themselves in the private sector, want to share their experience in public service, and perhaps in the process become a historic figure. This is yet another strain of Potomac fever—one that can be caught without actually crossing the Potomac. It is the nature of this malady to see little that is right about government and to see little that cannot be made right through the application of "sound business principles."

The difficulty with this approach, of course, is that government, with all its checks and balances, was not designed to be efficient, let alone businesslike. Nor should we want to sacrifice democracy for efficiency. Especially in a democracy, government is a process of compromising many diverse and conflicting interests, an inherently inefficient process. Many talented businesspeople have left the private sector to serve, honorably and well, in the highest government positions, yet government remains unbusinesslike. That should tell us something.

Business finance has little to do with government finance. As discussed above, the government is the people, and the people both owe the public debt and own the public debt. Put in accounting terms, the people collectively own both sides of the ledger. Also, government debt securities are ultimately backed by the government's taxing power and by its ability to create money. That is why U.S. Treasury bonds are always rated higher in the market than the best corporate bonds. Investors in Treasury securities are not worried about the safety of their principal (although all fixed-income debt instruments are subject to the devaluation of inflation and rising interest rates). Nevertheless, many businesspeople liken government debt to their own limited ability to borrow and conclude that the government is headed for financial ruin.

The general public gobbles up scary predictions of doom and gloom, especially if they are made by successful businesspeople, whom the American people tend to admire. The Ross Perot phenomenon is a good example of this public attitude, given that his central focus is the burden of the national debt on future generations. Another recent example is Harry Figgie, author of the 1992 book *Bankruptcy 1995*. In 1992, Figgie was chairman of Figgie International, then a major U.S. corporation. (The corporation reportedly came close to bankruptcy in 1994.)[2] Figgie's dire predictions about the financial condition of the U.S. government, culminating in bankruptcy in 1995, made no more sense when he wrote them than they do today, but his book was on the *New York Times* best-seller list for nine months.

An obvious part of the communications problem is that bad news drives out good news. People seem to prefer to believe the worst, especially when it comes to their government. It is certainly not popular to be bullish about the national debt, so the bad news bears have a field day.

The doomsayers in the private sector also include prominent clergymen who perpetuate the notion that debt constitutes an immoral legacy. One such writer, Robert Schuller, dedicated his book *The Power of Being Debt Free* to "our unborn children and grandchildren with the hope that someday they will be able to secure a thirty-year fixed-rate mortgage on their home at 7 percent."[3] In 1985, when the book was published, the new home mortgage rate was approximately

12 percent. In 1993 the rate got down to Schuller's hoped-for 7 percent, even though the gross federal debt had soared during this period, from $1.6 trillion in 1984 to $4.4 trillion in 1993.

THE POLITICAL ECONOMIST

When I speak to groups about the national debt, I am often asked why other economists have not expressed similar views.

Nearly all politicians on the national stage have the benefit of advice from economists who know, for example, that the alleged burden of the national debt on future generations is grossly exaggerated. Have these economists failed in their advisory function? Have they sought to ingratiate themselves by telling their political bosses only what they think they want to hear—that is, what they think the people want to hear? Have they resigned themselves to their perception of the current political correctness? Or have they provided good counsel but only in privileged executive communications not available for public disclosure? The correct answer, from my observations of many top economic advisers to the president, is "all of the above."

Actually, many academic economists have done a pretty good communications job, especially in the last decade. Prominent economists from several major universities and other private institutions have produced a number of popular books on the public debt written in understandable terms for the average reader.[4] Not surprisingly, they disagree among themselves, but they provide an excellent body of analysis in the process. What is surprising is the apparent certainty and agreement among politicians (from both major parties) on matters on which the experts strongly disagree.

Why do politicians ignore the experts? As one economist commenting on the Reagan administration deficits put it, the "increasingly familiar claim has been that . . . the policy of running up ever larger deficits and government debt . . . was not a failure of economic thinking but a carefully calculated plan for forcing the government to reduce its role in American life."[5]

Government economists (and many business economists) are generally expected to serve the chair they sit in. Thus the longstanding

Washington quip, "Where you stand on an issue depends on where you sit." The economic spokespersons for the various government agencies are usually subcabinet political appointees whose average tenure is only about two years. Their government service is just a brief interruption in a career in industry, banking, academe, or other parts of the private sector. During their terms in office they are expected to echo the views of the president, cabinet members, and other top officials of the administration they are committed to serve. This point was succinctly put by one secretary of the Treasury when explaining to his staff why they must support a presidential order they did not agree with: "I am a man of principle, and my first principle is to do what my boss tells me to do."

This is not to say that there is no individual responsibility. One must act legally and ethically. But when it comes to differences of opinion on policy matters, government officials must be responsive to the politicians elected by the people.

I recall one able assistant secretary who came to the Treasury from Wall Street and publicly embraced the Treasury's traditional negative view of tax breaks for certain municipal bonds. When he later returned to a Wall Street job in the municipal bond business, he openly opposed the Treasury's position. When asked about the apparent inconsistency in his views, he said simply, "I was born again."

Of course, many appointees have strongly held and well-known private views that are compatible with the policies of the president and are expected to be expressed in public. Many others are pragmatic and are happy to defend the current administration's policies, whatever they are and however they may change. Indeed, some have been viewed as enjoying the challenge of publicly defending administration policies with which they personally disagree. I remember well one brilliant deputy secretary of the Treasury who, after demolishing my argument that the Treasury should take a certain position on a piece of pending legislation, said, "What do you want me to do? I can argue it either way."

There have been occasions when political appointees have made public statements contrary to the views of the administration, inadvertently or otherwise. Generally that is not tolerated for very long. The people elect a president, not a bunch of economists or other technicians. If appointees cannot support their president, or at least remain silent when they disagree, they are expected to resign. This is especially true of economists and other social scientists whose fields abound with conflicting theories rather than scientific fact.

It is difficult to separate economics from politics. President Lyndon Johnson reportedly often instructed his aides to "Leave the politics to me." The classical term for economics is *political economy;* and the classical politician—that is, the representative of the people—may well make a better judgment as to how people will react to a particular policy or set of economic circumstances than an economist cloistered in an ivory tower. Politicians generally fancy themselves good judges of people and tend to rely on their intuition rather than defer to the judgment of economists. Politicians would sooner leave war to the generals than economics to the economists. (I do not mean to criticize political appointees. It was my privilege to serve under dozens of them during my three decades in the Treasury. They were different in many respects—Republicans and Democrats, conservatives and liberals, academics and hard-headed businesspeople, managers and technicians—but it was rare to find one who was not a person of honor and intelligence.)

THE WILL OF THE PEOPLE

Let us now consider why, then, our elected officials keep preaching nonsense about government debt, portraying the buildup of budget deficits as the financial equivalent of eating the seedcorn. Perhaps some actually believe what they say. Others, recognizing the need for greater control over government spending and deficits, may believe that need is best met by advancing any and all plausible arguments, however specious, against government deficits—in other words, the end justifies the means. Yet the apparent major reason why politicians continue to perpetuate these myths is simply that they have concluded that this is what the voters want to hear.

My earliest recollection of "tell them what they want to hear" politics comes in the form of a young and relatively innocent Treasury Department economist at a Florida convention of an association of investment bankers, most of whom were in the tax-exempt municipal bond business. A principal speaker to the convention was a prominent congressman who was a senior member of the House Ways and Means Committee, which had jurisdiction over matters such as tax exemption of municipal bonds. The Congressman made a spirited defense of the municipal bond business and its "well-deserved" tax benefits. After his speech, I was chatting with the president of the association, and I said that the Congressman seemed to have very strong views about tax-free municipal bonds. He responded that he did not know about that, but said that just before making his speech to the convention, the Congressman had asked him what the investment bankers wanted to hear. The association president said he told the Congressman about their interest in tax-exempt bonds, and the Congressman went ahead and delivered.

A popular Washington story about "tell them what they want to hear" politics arose after John Kennedy had defeated Richard Nixon for the presidency in 1960. The newly elected Kennedy and his staff were resting in Florida when Kennedy reportedly asked his staff, "What do we do now? What are the policies of our new administration?" A staff member reportedly responded that there was a guy in Washington, a senior career official in the Budget Bureau,[6] who had collected newspaper clippings on reports of Kennedy and Nixon campaign speeches throughout the country and arranged the clippings by subject in two thick loose-leaf books, one called a Jackopedia and the other a Dickopedia. After the election, the story went, the Dickopedia was discarded and the Jackopedia was retained to provide the Budget Bureau staff with some notion of what policy initiatives to expect from their new political bosses. Kennedy reportedly instructed his staff to bring the Budget Bureau official and his Jackopedia to Florida to help them get started on the task of framing a set of policies.

This process of forming national policy from campaign speeches, themselves based on what local leaders tell candidates the people want to hear, may well be criticized as followership rather than leadership, but it appears to be essential to political survival.

CONCLUSION

The myths about the national debt persist in part because of a lack of understanding of how public finance is inherently different from business or personal finance. Unlike private debt, the national debt is both an asset and a liability of virtually all the people. Political leaders have perpetuated the myths largely because it has been "politically correct" to do so. So long as the voters want to believe the myths, politicians will tell them what they want to hear.

10   The Reality: Spending Control

To PARAPHRASE AN OLD PRAYER: Give us the courage to control that which we can control, the serenity to accept that which we cannot control, and the wisdom to recognize the difference between the two. The reality of the federal budget and deficit is that we can control program costs, we cannot control interest costs, and the way to recognize the difference between the two in the budget is to include the former and exclude the latter.

THE NEED FOR ACCOUNTABILITY

The real reason we should hate the deficit is that politicians generally should not be able to increase government spending without increasing taxes. Politicians should not have the pleasure of spending (getting votes) without the pain of taxing (losing votes). We need that accountability to ensure that the spending is justified—that the taxpayers are willing to pay for it—and that there is a discipline over Washington's reallocation of the nation's economic resources. That's good government and good economics.

We also need to balance the budget to help restore confidence in government. Politicians scare people by ranting and raving about the evils of government deficits and debt. Then they get elected and do nothing about them. Government does some wonderful things, but if political leaders keep saying that our biggest problem is the national debt and then fail to do anything about it, voters understandably put them down as failures. Much of the public cynicism about government undoubtedly arises from the fact that for twenty-six years leaders of both political parties have failed to deliver on their promises to balance the budget. Even voters who may not worry much about the deficits conclude that politicians are liars or incompetents because they do not achieve what they (the politicians) say must be achieved.

Economist Herbert Stein put it this way in 1994: "Nothing better reveals the vacuum in economic policy than the gap between the nearly universal statements of aversion to budget deficits and the prospect of exceptionally large deficits for as far ahead as the eye can see. No one any longer talks about balancing the budget—the necessary action is considered worse than the deficit."[1] I assume Stein means that no one talks sincerely about balancing the budget in the near future. Indeed, since the 1994 congressional elections, balancing the budget has dominated the congressional debate, but it remains to be seen whether this budget talkathon will actually lead to significant deficit reduction. As Will Rogers said about the weather, "Everybody talks about it. Nobody does anything about it."

THE NEED FOR A "PROGRAM BUDGET"

Many economists think of the federal budget deficit or surplus as a tool of economic policy. That kind of thinking can get us into real trouble (as discussed below). The budget should be viewed not as an economic document but solely as a means of controlling government spending. There is no other means of control. No large organization, public or private, can operate efficiently without the discipline and accountability provided by a credible budget process.

So what do we do about the $5 trillion debt? Nothing. That's behind us. The focus now should be on controlling future spending. What about interest on the debt? We must pay it. We have no choice. Moreover, interest is not the spending problem we should be concerned about—no politician is buying votes by spending taxpayer money on interest on the debt.

Interest on the public debt should be treated in essentially the same way as other public debt receipts and expenditures. Government borrowings and repayments of past borrowings have never been included in the budget as receipts and expenditures. They are counted instead as "means of financing" the budget. If Congress does not provide enough taxes to pay the bills for the spending it has mandated, the government has no choice but to borrow. So it is with interest on the public debt. Once the borrowing is done, the interest must be paid. Accordingly, Congress has authorized a "permanent indefinite appropriation" (which is governmentese for "spend whatever and whenever is necessary") for interest on the public debt, and it is misleading to include interest in proposed budget expenditures. It is not proposed; it is already a done deal. Interest should be viewed, along with the principal repayments, as a necessary part of total debt service. Realistically, interest is a repayment of borrowing. As discussed in chapter 4, interest should not be confused with the program expenditures of the government. Any effort to minimize future additions to the public debt interest burden should be a part of a revised debt limit process proposed later in this chapter.

We need to narrow our budget focus to the real problem, the *program* deficit—that is, the current deficit less interest. Then our sight will be set on a meaningful goal—an achievable goal—to balance the program budget and to balance it now, not in the year 2002. Then we will have an effective measure by which to judge political performance and to subject government spending to the democratic process.

Does this mean that we should try to balance the program budget every year? Yes. By that I mean the program budget proposal submitted to Congress by the president in January of each year should show a balancing of receipts and expenditures, with a deficit or surplus near zero, except for interest, which should be estimated and shown separately. Then Congress should make its changes to the president's budget and enact the required appropriations legislation, which should also be calculated to result in a balanced program budget.

WHY UNPLANNED DEFICITS ARE OK

Would such an authorization process actually produce balanced budgets? No, of course not. No budget process can be designed to produce an actual balance in the budget. Most of the economic and other estimates on which the budget is based must be done well in advance of the budget year. Otherwise the budget could not be transmitted by the president soon enough to give Congress time to consider it and enact the necessary appropriations. As stated in the budget for fiscal year 1996: "The process of formulating the budget begins not later than the spring of each year, at least nine months before the budget is transmitted and at least 18 months before the fiscal year begins."[2]

By the end of the fiscal year, thirty months have elapsed since the budget formulation for that year began. During that period, economic changes, natural disasters, foreign problems, and other unanticipated events may have had substantial effects on both tax receipts and program expenditures. A well-known example is the unexpected economic recession, when incomes and thus tax receipts decrease and unemployment benefit payments increase, resulting in a significant budget deficit. Conversely, an unanticipated economic boom can produce a large budget surplus. A good, but not necessary, outcome would be an approximate budget balance over the course of the multiyear business cycle.

These deviations from annual balanced budgets should not be a concern. They are passive budget changes triggered by external forces, not by political decisions to give budget-busting tax breaks or new spending programs to favored constituents. In fact, such automatic changes in deficits and surpluses help stabilize the economy, particularly during a recession, when unemployment benefit payments and food stamps help to sustain incomes and consumer spending.

WHY PLANNED DEFICITS ARE NOT OK

This is not to say that the government should enact new tax cuts or spending programs—for example, for the construction of public facilities—during recessions to stimulate the economy. That has generally been counterproductive. The average recession over the last fifty years has lasted only about eleven months. For several reasons, we are generally into a recession before the recession is officially recognized: lags and errors in preliminary economic statistics, understandable wariness about possible false signals in the early months of a recession, and political reluctance to admit to weakness in the economy. By the time the recession is recognized and the tax reductions or spending increases are authorized, the average recession is nearly over. Then the actual impact of the economic stimulus—especially public works projects that require long lead times for planning, competitive bidding, and contracting procedures—generally occurs after the recession is over. This adds unwanted pressures and competition with private business for scarce resources during the ensuing economic recovery period.

It might be argued that tax reductions, unlike spending increases, could be timely enough to moderate a recession. There are two problems with that argument.

First, while the tax reduction would supply funds to the private economy, it would also cause an increase in government borrowing (assuming no change in government spending), which would drain funds from the private economy. Although tax reductions are likely to have somewhat more economic impact than borrowing, as discussed earlier, the impact is likely to be marginal compared with actual changes in government spending. Second, a tax change is simply a transfer of money. Only as the money is spent does it work its way through the economy and stimulate the creation of new jobs. So, in both cases, tax reduction and spending increases, economic recessions are simply too short to be susceptible to effective moderation by government countercyclical fiscal policies.

Also, the very prospect of increased federal funds for public facilities can cause delays in the initiation of new projects during a recession and further weaken the economy. Project sponsors would be alert to opportunities to delay construction with the hope that their projects would qualify later for the additional federal financial assistance.

Public facility construction is more likely to be a source of stability in the economy if it is distributed evenly over the years rather than turned on or off with the business cycle. Moreover, public facility construction proposals should be judged on their own merits as part of a sound long-term planning and development process rather than expedited on the basis of their alleged contribution to creating jobs during a recession.

Apart from the very effective built-in stabilizers, such as unemployment benefits, proposals for economic stimuli by the government during recessions should be rejected. Government does not have the know-how to time its activities to counter the business cycle and fine-tune the economy; even if it did, it would need to overcome formidable political obstacles to distribute spending on the basis of what is good for the country rather than what is demanded by vested political interests. Various interest groups see every economic slowdown as an opportunity to advocate more government spending for their particular cause or business. Have you noticed how many government buildings, bridges, and other public facilities are named after the member of Congress who managed to get that slice of the federal pork pie for his or her district?

A distinction should be made between the relatively mild and short-lived economic recessions we have had in the United States over the last fifty years and the severe and prolonged Great Depression of the 1930s. In that Depression, countercyclical fiscal policies made sense, including public works projects. But in the postwar period countercyclical fiscal policy became more a political exercise than an economic one. Economic planners on Washington ego trips, lobbyists grasping for their share of the pie, members of Congress eager to get more for their district—all added up to an image of excessive, meddling, "have money, will travel" government that gave Washington a bad name and achieved little or nothing toward the stated goal of moderating the business cycle.

Why should we care about all this ancient history? Surely we learn from experience and are not likely to repeat such obvious mistakes as activist countercyclical fiscal policies. Lest I be accused of fighting old wars, consider the following statement from President Clinton's Council of Economic Advisers: "The role that fiscal policy can play in smoothing fluctuations in the business cycle is one of the great discoveries of modern economics. Unfortunately, the huge deficits inherited from the last decade have made discretionary changes in fiscal policy in response to the business cycle all but impossible.

A balanced budget amendment would eliminate the automatic stabilizers as well, thus completely removing fiscal policy from the macroeconomic policy arsenal."[3] Apparently, the huge deficits did serve some useful purpose.

I agree with the council that a balanced budget amendment to the Constitution would be a mistake, but not for the reason stated by the council. (As shown above, discretionary countercyclical fiscal policies simply do not work, although I would agree with the council on the automatic stabilizers, such as unemployment compensation and food stamps.) Others have stated the much more important concern that a constitutional amendment would inevitably involve the courts in the current budget decisions of Congress and the president. That would be disastrous. In my view, the reason to hate the deficit is that it allows spending without taxation and thus without control by the people. Turning the federal budget over to judges who are appointed for life and are thus not even subject to the vote of the people is clearly not the way to go. Also, after three decades of dealing with presidential and congressional budget gimmickry, I am convinced that there is no way to draft an effective constitutional amendment to balance the budget. The amendment would need to be flexible enough to deal with budget emergencies and economic changes; and it would be so complex—dealing with the endless federal accounting niceties that have been the refuge of the budget scoundrels—that it would be virtually incomprehensible to the people and to the states that would need to ratify it.

The fiscal activism in the above statement by President Clinton's economists reflects the thinking of many economists when I first came to Washington back in the 1950s, but it has since been discredited. It is a totally unrealistic notion that the government can actually fine-tune the economy and moderate the business cycle by making discretionary adjustments in government taxing and spending. This misguided view led to the enactment of the Public Works Acceleration Act in 1962, which authorized federal spending for public facility projects throughout the country during periods of economic recession.[4] That legislation was clearly counterproductive, as recognized in a recent report by economist Bruce Bartlett: "the peak number of

jobs created came in June 1964, 37 months after the recession bot-
tomed out." In that same report, Bartlett concludes, "All postwar
countercyclical programs were enacted after the recessions' end. They
exacerbated inflation, raised interest rates and made the next recession
worse."[5]

Economist Laurence Kotlikoff made a similar criticism of government fine-tuning in 1992:

> There are two problems with fine-tuning. First, it takes Congress
> time to pass new fiscal legislation, with the result that when the
> new laws take effect the problem they were meant to fix may
> no longer exist. A second and more fundamental concern was
> identified by the University of Chicago economists Robert Lucas
> and Thomas Sargent. Lucas and Sargent pointed out that the
> public will catch on to the government's fine-tuning policies
> and wait for these policies to be enacted before responding.
> Thus if the country is in a recession and everyone expects the
> government to, say, subsidize new investment to stimulate eco-
> nomic activity, business will hold off on its investment until
> those subsidies are enacted. This waiting game, of course, lowers
> investment during the presubsidy period and, as a consequence,
> makes the shortfall in investment, and the recession, that much
> worse.[6]

The public behavior described by economists Lucas and Sargent in
the above quote has become known as *rational expectations,* and in
1995 Robert Lucas was awarded the Nobel Prize for economics for
his work in this area. The Royal Swedish Academy of Sciences said
in its citation that Lucas "had made the most important contribution
to the field of macroeconomics since the 1970s, when he pioneered
what is now called the 'rational expectations' school."[7]

No judgment is made in this analysis as to whether the current level
of government spending is too much or too little. Personally, I think
it's intolerable that the richest country in the world acts as if it cannot
afford to fill its potholes, repair its crumbling bridges, replace its burst-
ing water mains, and eliminate other daily reminders of our deteriorat-
ing public facilities. I would be happy to pay more taxes to fix our

infrastructure, but that's just one man's view. Whatever the appropriate level of government spending, it must be subject to the discipline that only a budget can provide. That discipline must be a requirement that proposed expenditures not exceed estimated receipts.

THE *WRONG* REASONS TO REDUCE THE DEFICIT

How does this approach to the federal budget deficit compare with the current approach of the President's Council of Economic Advisers? Not very well. The council's approach is stated in the following excerpt from the 1995 *Economic Report of the President:*

> Perhaps the most important reason for reducing the federal budget deficit is to increase national saving. . . .
>
> A second reason for reducing the deficit is to reduce the debt burden that the present generation will bequeath to future generations. . . . yet it is important not to overstate the problem or to use it as an excuse to skimp on public investment. We also bequeath to future generations a stock of physical capital—highways, airports, and the like—as well as a stock of human capital and technological knowledge. Because these add importantly to future generations' productivity and well-being, these assets will somewhat reduce their debt burden.
>
> A third reason is that a large deficit hamstrings discretionary fiscal policy as a tool of macroeconomic stabilization. In the presence of a looming deficit, it is difficult for the Federal Government to respond to cyclical slowdowns by cutting taxes or increasing spending. A gradual policy of reducing deficits can build a cushion in case the Federal Government needs to engage in countercyclical fiscal policy sometime in the future.[8]

So my suggested reason for hating the federal budget deficit—spending control—did not make the council's top three reasons for deficit reduction; indeed I found no indication in the report that it would even make the council's top ten. Again, I am not arguing for less government spending, or more. I don't know how much government we should have. But there must be a means of controlling spending. (Surely no one would argue that spending should be out of control.) The only means of control is a requirement to balance the budget; that way, the control over spending will come from the natural taxpayer resistance to paying for any more government than necessary. (Surely no one would argue for unnecessary government.)

Let us consider the council's three reasons for deficit reduction.

The first reason, to increase national saving, reflects the fact that the federal deficit is shown in our national accounts as dissaving, regardless of the amount of government investment. If an individual borrows money to buy a house, the borrowing, or dissaving, is generally more than offset by the investment in the house, and the net effect is generally a small increase in personal saving. Similarly, business borrowing, say to build a new factory, is reflected as an increase in financial liabilities and an offsetting increase in physical assets. Yet similar government investments are treated as if they were current operating expenses.

In fiscal year 1995, the government's deficit was $164 billion and its reported new investments were much larger at $237 billion.[9] (This does not include most spending on national security or various education or other programs that some would regard as our greatest investments in the future.) Net investment (after depreciation) is not shown, or known; if it were, that would be the proper "businesslike" measure of government investment or saving, regardless of whether the investment were financed by borrowing from the private sector or by taxing the private sector. As discussed in chapter 2, what counts most is how the government spends the money, not how the money was raised.

The council's second reason for reducing the deficit, to reduce the alleged intergenerational debt burden, was also dealt with in chapter 2. To its credit, the council recognizes that government investment in physical and human capital "will somewhat reduce" the debt burden on future generations (so the council apparently recognizes that its concern that the federal deficit reduces saving would be alleviated to the extent that the deficit is incurred to increase investment). Yet the council does not recognize that future generations will also inherit assets, in the form of Treasury securities, which will offset their national debt liabilities. The net effect is that future generations are benefitted, not burdened, by today's budget to the extent that the budget provides for a net investment in physical or human resources.

The third reason, that the deficit "hamstrings discretionary fiscal policy," has no merit and was dealt with earlier in this chapter. The notion that the government can adjust spending and taxation to moderate the business cycle has been discredited, largely because economic recessions do not last long enough to be affected by the delayed economic impact of proposed tax and spending changes. Because of their lagged effects and their inherently political and inefficient nature, such emergency measures do more harm than good.

Economists, both liberals and conservatives, point to statistics such as taxes or spending as a percentage of gross domestic product as if there were some way to determine the "right" size of government from historical statistics, comparisons with other countries, cost/benefit analyses, or some foggy concepts of "public" versus "private" goods. Such analyses are helpful to our understanding of our society, but they are of limited value in determining what government should or should not do.

In a democracy, there is only one way to determine the proper function or size of government: government must be whatever the people want it to be. The only way to know how much government the people want is to determine how much they are willing to pay for, and the only way to know that is to limit spending to the amount of taxes levied, that is, to balance the budget. Indeed, there is no other budget policy that is compatible with a democratic form of government. Again, as discussed earlier, if we have another Great Depression or world war, all bets are off. But there has been no event in the past fifty years, in my view, that would have justified departure from the balanced budget policy suggested here.

THE INADEQUACY OF ALTERNATIVE BUDGET PRESENTATIONS

Many alternative budget presentations have been proposed by economists—again, both liberals and conservatives—seeking to devise a better measure of the impact of the government on the economy.

While these measures serve various purposes (as discussed below), no one of them is an improvement over the present unified budget from the standpoint of the central purpose of controlling government spending.

The Unified Budget.   The official budget is the so-called unified budget, which generally measures cash receipts and expenditures of agencies owned in whole or in part by the U.S. government. The unified budget was developed by the President's Commission on Budget Concepts in 1967 and was first implemented in fiscal year 1969. Since then, legislation has been enacted to take many agencies or programs out of the unified budget, but most of them were later put back. Congressional decisions to exclude certain entities from the discipline of the budget are based on political considerations rather than the nature of the entity. The only exclusions now are the Social Security retirement and disability funds (the Medicare fund is not excluded) and the Postal Service fund. They are designated as "off-budget" federal entities and are exempt from certain budget constraints imposed on other federal entities, but their transactions are added to the totals of the on-budget entities to arrive at the total deficit figures that are the focus of the balanced budget debates in Congress today.

If all this sounds irrational, it is. The purpose of the President's Commission on Budget Concepts was to restore public confidence in the budget, which had seriously eroded because of the perception of excessive budget gimmickry by the Johnson administration.[10] The commission was widely hailed as one of the most successful presidential commissions, but the ink was barely dry on its report before special exemptions were granted to various favored entities.

While I doubt that a completely credible federal budget can ever be achieved—especially given my experience in providing staff support to the President's Commission on Budget Concepts—I am pleased to note that the federal budget is probably a more credible document today than it has been for many decades. Major changes in the budget treatment of loans and loan guarantees (to report their costs in terms of the present value of their subsidies), proposed by the Treasury staff in 1967, were finally adopted by Congress in the Federal Credit Reform Act of 1990. While certain programs are exempt from the overall budget constraints, they are included in the total deficit figures, which facilitates disclosure of the full range of federal spending programs. There will probably always be some "off-budget" programs that are exempt from certain controls for political reasons, but there now seems to be an accepted practice of at least including their transactions in the budget totals and focusing on that "total" budget in the national discussions and debates over federal budget policy.

The National Income and Product Budget. Many economists prefer the National Income and Product (NIPA) budget, which is developed by the Commerce Department to provide a better measure of the economic impact of the government's budget, consistent with the overall structure of the national income and product accounts for the private sector. The NIPA budget is included as background information in the budget documents submitted to Congress each year. It excludes certain lending, deposit insurance, and other financial transactions that are included in the unified budget, and it has thus shown somewhat smaller deficits in recent years. The NIPA budget also differs from the unified budget in format and in the timing of certain transactions, differences that have only minor effects on the size of the reported budget deficit. The NIPA budget has not received much attention in the current debate over balancing the budget or controlling federal spending.

More Liberal Budgets. Some economists, for example, Robert Eisner and Robert Heilbroner,[11] say that the official federal budget figures greatly overstate the "real" government deficit. They, along with other liberal economists, suggest a number of adjustments that would reduce the government deficit and provide what they believe would be a better measure of government's fiscal impact on the economy. These adjustments include adding the state and local government surpluses to the federal budget deficit, reducing the deficit by the amount of federal investments (a capital budget concept), and reducing the deficit by the amount that the federal debt burden is reduced by inflation. Such adjustments are substantial. For example, Heilbroner's recalculation of the fiscal year 1988 budget deficit reduced it from the official figure of $255 billion to an "operating" budget deficit of just $3 billion.[12]

More Conservative Budgets. More conservative economists would go in the other direction and add to the official unified budget deficits such enormous amounts as the multitrillion-dollar actuarial deficits in Social Security, Medicare, and other federal trust funds, as well as certain contingent liabilities of the government, including FHA-insured home mortgages, FDIC-insured bank deposits, and other guaranteed and insured loans and deposits. A difficulty with this approach is determining where to stop. The government also faces other large contingencies, such as natural disaster relief and unemployment benefit payments. Should we have had a reserve for the bailouts of New York City and the Chrysler Corporation? The greatest financial risks to the government, at least during times of peace, are the inevitable economic recessions, during which tax revenues decrease and economic assistance payments increase; but these risks are no more susceptible to quantification in the government's financial statements than the risks of future military costs to deal with unexpected threats to our national interests. The major financial risks faced by the government cannot be reflected adequately in an accounting statement.

The Full-Employment Budget. There are various other ways that economists recalculate the federal budget deficit, including the full-employment, or "structural," deficit, which is calculated to exclude that portion of the unified budget deficit or surplus attributable to the business cycle and thus to provide a better measure of the longer-run deficit problem and of the impact of budget policy on the economy. Currently, there is no significant difference between the unified deficit and the structural deficit, as calculated by the Office of Management and Budget, because the economy is close to full employment.[13]

The Capital Budget. There are also many different ways of developing a capital budget, as discussed in chapter 2, depending on the treatment of such long-term investments as fixed capital, equipment, research and development, and education and training. The Office of Management and Budget, while not endorsing a capital budget, provides an extensive analysis of federal investment spending and capital budgeting in its 1996 budget presentation.[14]

Generational Accounting.   The most recent, and perhaps most radical, alternative budget presentation is called generational accounting, which attempts to measure the relative fiscal burden of government, including state and local governments, on current and future generations. Generational accounting was developed in 1991 by three economists who presented it as an alternative to the government's present deficit accounting approach.[15] It is an ambitious undertaking that employs present value analysis in developing measures of the impact that today's budget decisions will have on the tax burden carried by future generations. The analysis must rely on extremely subjective and debatable economic and policy assumptions, including critical assumptions on inflation and interest rates. Also, generational accounting assumes that the national debt is a burden on future generations, contrary to my analysis in chapter 2. While generational accounting has not been accepted by the Office of Management and Budget or by the Congressional Budget Office as an alternative or supplement to the government's budget accounts, those offices have encouraged its future development as a tool for analyzing the long-term impact of the budget.[16]

Each of the above budget concepts serves a useful purpose in furthering understanding of the impact of government on our society. But no one of them is an improvement over the unified budget now in use, when judged from the standpoint of controlling federal spending. It has been argued that the unified budget is not an adequate control vehicle because it does not include the full cost of long-term commitments to such programs as Social Security, Medicare, and other pension and insurance programs. Yet these "commitments" are not cast in stone. They have been reduced, and probably will be reduced further by new legislation currently under consideration. The only truly uncontrollable budget item of any consequence is interest on the public debt, which is one of the reasons why the budget treatment of interest should be changed.

IMPLEMENTATION OF THE
PROGRAM BUDGET

Table 10-1 compares the actual (unified) budget deficit with the proposed program budget deficit for the fiscal years 1970–1995. The unified budget was in deficit in each of these twenty-six years. The program budget showed a deficit in all but five of these years, and the only large surplus was the $68.3 billion in fiscal year 1995. The budget estimates submitted by the president in March 1996 shows declining unified budget deficits for fiscal years 1995–2000 and surpluses for 2001–2002. (On that basis, there would be a program budget surplus in each of these seven years.)

The president's "rosy scenario," however, has been greeted with considerable skepticism, and his new budget proposals were pronounced "dead on arrival" at Capitol Hill. It is generally recognized that unified budget deficits will actually increase in the next decade, absent legislation to curb the growth in health expenditures. Indeed, it seems likely that there will be chronic deficits even in the program budget, as was the case in seventeen of the past twenty years (which is why it is important to take advantage of the current window of opportunity to commit to balance in the new program budget).

The president should announce a policy of establishing now, as a minimum requirement, the elimination of that portion of the deficit that is controllable (that is, the current deficit less net interest). This would provide a realistic goal (already achieved in fiscal year 1995), which would not be frustrated by variations in market interest rates and uncontrollable interest expenditures.

Second, the commitment to a balanced program budget should be accompanied by a proposal by the president that Congress adopt a new public debt authorization process that would ensure a more timely annual focus and debate on the appropriate size of the debt and the program budget surplus, if any. Each year a balanced program budget would be approved, along with any surplus amount deemed appropriate to reduce the growth of the national debt. There would be no need to create a special fund for deficit or debt reduction; any reductions would be achieved automatically by the amounts of the

Table 10-1 Unified budget deficit and program budget deficit, fiscal years 1970–1995

Year	Unified deficit	Net interest	Program deficit (−)/surplus	Year	Unified deficit	Net interest	Program deficit (−)/surplus
1970	−2.8	14.4	11.6	1983	−207.8	89.8	−118.0
1971	−23.0	14.8	−8.2	1984	−185.4	111.1	−74.3
1972	−23.4	15.5	−7.9	1985	−212.3	129.5	−82.8
1973	−14.9	17.3	2.4	1986	−221.2	136.0	−85.2
1974	−6.1	21.4	15.3	1987	−149.8	138.7	−11.1
1975	−53.2	23.2	−30.0	1988	−155.2	151.8	−3.4
1976	−73.7	26.7	−47.0	1989	−152.5	169.3	16.8
1977	−53.7	29.9	−23.8	1990	−221.4	184.2	−37.2
1978	−59.2	35.5	−23.7	1991	−269.2	194.5	−74.7
1979	−40.2	42.6	2.4	1992	−290.4	199.4	−91.0
1980	−73.8	52.5	−21.3	1993	−255.1	198.8	−56.3
1981	−79.0	68.8	−10.2	1994	−203.2	203.0	−.2
1982	−128.0	85.0	−43.0	1995	−163.9	232.2	68.3

Source: Derived from Office of Management and Budget, Budget of the United States Government, Fiscal Year 1993, Supplement (Washington, D.C.: GPO, 1992), 19–20, 39–42; Office of Management and Budget, Budget of the United States Government, Fiscal Year 1995 (Washington, D.C.: GPO, 1994), 235; Office of Management and Budget, Analytical Perspectives, Budget of the United States Government, Fiscal Year 1997 (Washington, D.C.: GPO, 1996), 189, 370.

program budget surpluses. Yet the separate and early focus on debt authorization would force Congress to face up to the public debt implications of their proposed spending decisions, *before* authorizing the spending, and would encourage an annual debate that could contribute to broader understanding of public finance. (The need for a change in the debt limit process is discussed in detail below.)

Accordingly, the president's March 1996 budget proposals for a fiscal year 1996 unified budget deficit of $146 billion and net interest outlays of $241 billion would be presented as a proposed program budget surplus of $95 billion. How much should the surplus be? The answer might depend on judgments of the appropriate size of the debt, interest on the debt, or the amount of net new borrowing by the Treasury.

This approach would change the focus of the debate. The budget would be viewed as a means of controlling the process of authorizing new spending. The debt limit, no longer a meaningless rubber stamp, would be an effective means of dealing with the financial effects of past as well as future spending.

The economic, financial, and budget effects of debt and interest are highly technical matters, and a broad bipartisan consensus would be essential to obtaining widespread public support and budget credibility. This might best be achieved by a bipartisan commission, including the chair and ranking members of the House and Senate Budget and Appropriations Committees, the secretary of the Treasury, the director of the Office of Management and Budget, the chair of the Council of Economic Advisers, and accounting and budget experts from the private sector. This was the approach taken in 1967 by the President's Commission on Budget Concepts, which was widely praised for developing a new unified budget and restoring the budget credibility so needed at that time.

The establishment of a new bipartisan commission (after the 1996 elections) on budget concepts could help resolve many of the public concerns raised in recent years by the excessive partisan bickering over the deficit, debt, Social Security financing, and other related issues. (The only major presidential initiative on budget reform since 1967 apparently was an interagency task force chaired by President Reagan's counsel, Peter Wallison, in 1986.)[17]

The debt reform proposed here should not be confused with previous debt or deficit reduction *funds,* which have been little more than political cosmetics. The most recent example is described in the following excerpt from President Clinton's budget for fiscal year 1996:

> On August 4, 1993, the President issued Executive Order 12858 to guarantee that the net deficit reduction achieved by the Omnibus Budget Reconciliation Act (OBRA) of 1993 is dedicated exclusively to reducing the deficit. The order established the Deficit Reduction Fund and requires that amounts equal to the spending reductions and revenue increases resulting from OBRA be credited to the Fund. . . .
>
> The order requires that the fund balances be used exclusively to redeem maturing debt obligations of the Treasury held by foreign governments.[18]

That is truly an extraordinary statement. How could "net deficit reduction" be anything but "reducing the deficit"? If funds intended for deficit reduction were diverted for other purposes, there would not be any "net deficit reduction."

As to the second requirement, that the new fund be used "exclusively" to redeem maturing Treasury debt held by foreign governments, what does that mean? All Treasury debt, held by foreigners or anyone else, must be redeemed at maturity. That's the nature of the contract. Setting up a new deficit reduction fund or any other kind of fund does not change anything. Actually, so long as we are just reducing the deficit, not the debt, all maturing debt must be refunded with new debt issues. Moreover, the amount of Treasury debt held by foreign governments will continue to be determined by the foreign governments themselves. The new fund will not change that either.

As discussed in chapter 6, the investment in Treasury securities by foreign governments is not a problem for the United States, and it is probably a net benefit. Yet the above statement from the President's budget seems to pander to the latent xenophobia of the American people by creating an image of evil empires about to evict us on Christmas Eve for nonpayment of our debts.

In short, the new deficit reduction fund does absolutely nothing, and it apparently was not intended to do anything. One can only conclude that the establishment of the fund was based on the cynical assumption that the American people are easily fooled by such cosmetics.[19]

My initial reaction to the fund was resentment at such an insult to people's intelligence. But then I could not help but be amused by the presentation. Here we have the Clinton administration saying that the "exclusive" purpose of the President's major legislative initiative in 1993 to achieve $500 billion in deficit reduction—which to this day is touted as the greatest achievement of the administration—is to reduce the amount of Treasury debt held by foreign governments. The new fund clearly does not accomplish that purpose, and there is no logical reason why we should want it to. On the one hand, the United States and Japan went to great lengths in 1995 to moderate the historic free fall in the value of the U.S. dollar relative to the Japanese yen. The Japanese cooperated in this effort by buying American dollars and thus supporting their value. So the Japanese invested their added dollars in U.S. Treasury securities, and we welcomed that. On the other hand, we say in effect that the primary purpose of federal deficit reduction is to redeem such Treasury security holdings by foreign governments. It seems the right hand does not know what the left hand is writing in the President's budget.

THE NEED FOR A TIMELIER
DEBT LIMIT PROCESS

The statutory debt limit is the means by which Congress exercises its power under Section 8 of Article 1 of the Constitution: "To borrow Money on the Credit of the United States." The current timing of congressional debt limit action—after Congress appropriates program funds and requires that they be spent—is too late to have any effect. Congress has thus relinquished its responsibility for the public debt. Why has Congress done this? Possibly because it is so eager to spend (getting votes) and so reluctant to tax (losing votes) that it is hesitant to face the inevitable debt consequences of its deficit spending. So it waits until the program spending is safely committed before "grudg-ingly" enacting the required debt increase, as if the increase were somebody else's fault. But from my observations, the major reason Congress delays action on the debt limit is that Congress prefers to use that limit for purposes other than limiting the debt. The only way Congress can carry out its responsibility to exercise control over the debt is to act on the debt limit legislation in time to have an effect—that is, when it appropriates the funds for the spending that will require the additional debt issuance. Until that happens, the debt limit will remain a farce.

The House of Representatives already has a debt limit process that ties in with the appropriations process (except that the House suspended its process in the fiscal year 1996 debt limit negotiations). Generally, when it passes its appropriations legislation, the House specifies the amount of the increase in the public debt that will be needed to fund its recommendations. House members are thus forced to face up to the inevitable debt consequences of their spending actions. Under my proposal they would continue with this process but would also specify the amount, if any, of the program budget surplus.

The Senate, unlike the House, now waits to deal with the need to increase the public debt limit until long after members vote the appropriations bills that create the need for the additional debt. So the vote on the debt limit is meaningless. It's too late. Congress has already mandated more spending than taxes, so the public debt must increase. The Treasury is faced with breaking one law or another: not spending what Congress ordered it to spend or exceeding the authorized debt limit. Everyone knows that the debt limit will be increased. The alternative of having the United States default on its debt and other obligations is not acceptable to anyone. The politicians responsible for that would likely be thrown out of office.

But the Senate likes to use the debt limit bill as an opportunity for self-righteous speech making about fiscal rectitude and as a vehicle for irrelevant legislative amendments that might otherwise be vetoed by the president. So the debt limit bill is frequently held hostage until the eleventh hour, just before the Treasury is expected to run out of the money it needs to send out the monthly Social Security checks and other politically sensitive payments.

During each of these many debt limit crises—I participated in fifty-five debt limit increases during my thirty-two years in the Treasury—the Treasury and other government agencies are forced to take extraordinary and costly actions to conserve cash and postpone borrowings to avoid exceeding the debt limit. The crisis will sometimes last for weeks as the Treasury gradually runs out of money to meet its obligations. Congressional leaders and the highest officials in the Treasury and in the Executive Office of the President become involved in day-to-day monitoring and micromanagement of the timing of the flows of billions of dollars of government receipts and expenditures that will determine the precise date by which the Congress must act to prevent default on the public debt or other obligations. Other serious business of the government is pushed aside as top political appointees, whose average tenure is only about two years, take a crash course in the intricate minutiae of public finance and bean counting that is generally left to the accountants. At least for these newcomers, the process is educational and, for some, actually exciting. For career Treasury staff, who have been through similar debt limit crises dozens of times, it is a mind-numbing exercise in futility.

It becomes a game of "chicken," with congressional staff suspicious of the Treasury's estimates of when it runs out of money and Treasury staff warning of the dire consequences of further delay. In fact, no one knows when the "drop dead" date will be. The cash estimates are always uncertain because of the enormous detail and complexity of the many daily transactions of the various agencies of the government throughout the world. Moreover, the Treasury would not actually "drop dead" at some point. Instead, it would have a lingering death, somewhat akin to a Chinese water torture.

First, the Treasury announces that it might have to postpone or cancel some of its regular weekly or monthly security auctions (see table 4-1) if Congress does not act soon to increase the debt limit. That creates a lot of uncertainty as investors and other market participants, including foreigners, need to prepare to adjust to alternative investments while they wait for further pronouncements from Washington.

Then, as the Treasury is forced to reschedule or cancel auctions, small investors with direct accounts with the Treasury must be notified that their scheduled investments or reinvestments in new Treasury issues will not be made.[20] Elderly widows, who are often afraid to keep their life savings in anything but short-term Treasury securities, become confused and frightened as they discover they will be losing interest as they wait to reinvest. They now need to make decisions on short notice about alternative investments they do not understand; no one can tell them when, or even if, Congress will act to end the crisis. All they know is that the government is in some kind of financial trouble and their investments are not as secure as they thought they were.

Meanwhile, back in Washington, eyes glaze over as Treasury tries to explain to Congress the seriousness of the investors' problems and the millions of dollars in costs to the Treasury from the administrative expenses, lost customers, and market disruption caused by the failure of Congress to act. But puny millions of dollars of government costs don't even register on the priority scales of a Congress dealing with budgets of hundreds of billions. Senate staffers reassure their senators, and the press, that Treasury is crying wolf, that it can always find lots of measures to take to avoid default.

In fact, there are many things Treasury can do to buy more time. It depends on how much damage can be tolerated. During such debt limit crises Treasury has often frustrated small investors by suspending the sales of U.S. savings bonds, disinvested certain government trust funds, manipulated other federal agency borrowing or investment activities, and resorted to many other costly and wasteful measures to avoid breaking the debt limit law. Treasury also has a long emergency planning list of other actions it can take, including selling the gold in Fort Knox and other government assets to raise cash without borrowing.

There is no answer to the question, "How long can the Treasury hold out without an increase in the debt limit?" There is no end to the foolish and irresponsible things that could be done. The process has never been fully tested. At some point the incumbent Secretary of the Treasury (after consulting quietly with the White House and congressional leaders) draws a line in the sand beyond which, he says, Treasury will not go. (Different secretaries draw the line at different places.) In what he hopes will be his final debt limit crisis letter to congressional leaders, the secretary asserts that if Congress does not act by X hour the United States, for the first time in history, will default.

Then Congress acts. The mock battle is over, and everyone puts away his debt limit briefing book until next year.

What's wrong with this? It's a farce. It's politics at its worst. It's government at its worst. It's a circus. The main attraction is the small group of principals in Congress, the Treasury, and the White House who must decide when the game is over. It may be over when negotiations conclude on an amendment attached to the debt limit bill that has absolutely nothing to do with the debt limit or when the the players sense that elderly voters are alarmed at the prospect of a delay in their Social Security checks. Or it may be over when they get bored with the game.

This circus also has a couple of side shows. There is the Treasury and other government staff, including political appointees who normally have a sizeable impact on policy matters but recognize that the debt limit exercise is 100 percent political and that their function is essentially damage control. They are reduced to tracking the numbers and getting answers to the many accounting, legal, and market questions raised as the Treasury is forced to consider one ridiculous dodge after another.

The other side show is a sort of debt limit cottage industry of economists and other technicians, mainly from Wall Street, who watch the Treasury cash flows and try to outguess other market participants as to what's playing at the Treasury staff sideshow—whether the Treasury will issue or cancel this or that bond or note as it tries to cope with the debt limit crisis. Some of these experts are former Treasury or Federal Reserve employees who have an insider's perspective on which numbers or alternative financing gimmicks to track. They serve a sort of discovery function in the market at times, but often miss the important point that the final resolution of a debt limit crisis is a matter of political tactics, rather than a financial or accounting matter.

The entire process does not reduce the public debt by 1 cent. In fact, the debt is enlarged by the millions of dollars of costs incurred during the crisis. Millions of investors have been frustrated and have lost money and confidence in the U.S. government. Dozens of highly placed politicians and officials have neglected the serious issues of the day and the needs of the American people while they took time out to play the politically self-serving debt limit game.

That public-be-damned attitude is not becoming to Congress and is certainly not what our country's founders had in mind. But then we see those same politicians on TV bemoaning the fact that Congress has slipped again in the public opinion polls. What do they expect? I have great respect for our elected representatives in Congress. They are generally a very able, dedicated, and public-spirited body, but at debt limit crisis times I think there ought to be some way to find Congress in "Contempt of Public."

THE 1996 DEBT LIMIT CRISIS

The Washington follies over the debt limit reached new heights in fiscal year 1996, but not because of any significant change in the behavior of the Treasury about avoiding exceeding the debt limit.

There was much partisan criticism of the Treasury for not complying with the legal requirement to issue public debt securities to the Civil Service Retirement Fund and to the G Fund of the Thrift Savings Plan. (Such investments would have consumed the debt issuance authority, which the Treasury used instead to issue debt in the market to raise funds to pay the government's bills.) Yet the Treasury had done the same thing several times in debt limit crises under previous administrations. Moreover, the safety and earnings of the funds were not threatened in any way, contrary to what the critics suggested. Many years earlier, Congress had enacted laws to ensure that if these funds ever lost earnings from lack of investment during a debt limit crisis they would be made whole by a restoration of earnings after the crisis. This "make whole" provision was first enacted for the Civil Service Retirement Fund and later, at my request, for the G Fund. I knew from my earlier Treasury experience that the guarantee would be essential to protect the investment earnings of plan participants.

The losers in the debt limit crisis were the taxpayers, who were out the millions of dollars of administrative expenses, the untold costs from disruption of the government securities market, and the costs of inaction on other vital legislation while congressional leaders were preoccupied with the all-consuming tactical maneuvering over the debt limit. These costs, coupled with the hundreds of millions of dollars of costs from the concurrent shutdown of the government for three weeks (while paying employees for staying home), may well be the most lasting popular impression of the 103rd Congress.

Apart from the above costs, the 1996 debt limit crisis was beset with problems far more serious than any I encountered during my Treasury tenure.

It was the first time that one of the major players, Speaker of the House Newt Gingrich, actually threatened to force the Treasury to default on the public debt obligations of the United States.[21]

It was the first time that highly respected private participants in the government securities market actually urged Congress to default rather than give in on its budget fight with the president. Some bond traders reportedly said, "Oh God, if rates go back up at all (because of default fears), it just gives us an opportunity to buy."[22] (The leading spokesman for that Wall Street group later changed his mind, saying default "would be tragic."[23])

It was the first time that a major bond rating agency, Moody's Investors Service Inc., put debt securities of the U.S. Treasury on "review for possible downgrade," because the debt limit struggle "significantly increased the risk of a default."[24]

Republican leaders later hurried to make clear that default was unthinkable and "was not on the table." Sanity prevailed. Some arrogant bond traders learned a political lesson. Newt Gingrich and other Republican leaders learned a market lesson, most of all not to listen to self-serving bond traders. While great damage may have been done to their reputations, it is hoped that no permanent damage was done to the credit of the United States that their predecessors worked so hard to establish over the past 200 years.

The most serious consequences of a default, or near default, on U.S. debt obligations are not the inevitable government and market disruption or the additional interest cost the Treasury might have to pay on its future borrowing; it is the undermining of confidence in the leadership of the United States in the eyes of its citizens and by foreign governments. If our government is so divided that it cannot function on the preservation of its own credit, how can it be trusted to honor its other obligations, foreign or domestic?

Surely, we can improve on the debt limit process.

CONCLUSION

To sum up, the real reason we should hate the deficit is that politicians should not have the pleasure of spending (getting votes) without the pain of taxing (losing votes). Without that discipline, federal spending is out of control.

The sole purpose of the federal budget should be to control federal spending. The budget should not be a vehicle for discretionary actions to moderate the business cycle; they do not work and they undermine spending control.

The only effective means of budget control is to require that federal spending proposals not exceed estimated receipts. Such a balanced budget requirement would ensure the budget discipline provided by politically unpopular tax increases.

To achieve such a balanced budget discipline, the budget should be redefined as a new "program budget," which would exclude interest on the public debt. Interest is uncontrollable, and it has grown so large that its inclusion in the budget makes it impossible to ensure a budget discipline over program spending; it also provides too much temptation to politicians to engage in budget gimmickry by making unrealistically low interest rate forecasts or mismanaging the public debt. The exclusion of interest would be an important step toward greater truth in budgeting.

Congressional focus on public debt interest should be in conjunction with a revised debt limit process, since the debt decisions dictate the interest requirements. For the debt limit to be meaningful, it must be acted on much earlier, at the time Congress authorizes the spending that determines the Treasury's borrowing needs. This would require

Congress to focus on the financial impact of its spending decisions in time to mandate any program budget surplus deemed necessary to reduce that impact.

Since these proposed changes in the budget and debt limit processes would be confusing to the public and would be subject to partisan political attacks, they should be considered by a bipartisan presidential commission.

Because I spent most of my working life in the Treasury Department, many of my friends and acquaintances are pretty conservative on the economic issues of the day, including the issue of government deficits and debt. Some of them have reacted to my ideas for this book with the following warning: "I don't disagree with the points that you're making, but aren't you concerned that downplaying the importance of the national debt might make it even more difficult to restrain those who would continue to run up irresponsible deficits?"

Good question. I am tempted to respond that the present approach of overstating the importance of the debt certainly has not worked to eliminate deficit spending, and it would be hard to make the present mess any messier. Yet it may well be that deficit spending would have been worse without the fear of the debt, however baseless that fear. I don't know.

What I do know is that no one is happy with the present confusion. Conservatives are anxious about an imagined national debt problem that will never be resolved. Liberals bemoan the interruption of social progress in the name of debt reduction that is never achieved. The millions of people in between—federal, state, and local government workers, government contractors, program beneficiaries—who provide or receive government services are partially "on hold," unable to plan or operate efficiently as government programs are turned on and off and then on again.

I also know that the stakes in this game are higher than ever, and I for one am not comfortable with a game plan based on continued bluffing. Perhaps we should give truth a chance. As the fellow said, "When in doubt, do the right thing."

NOTES

INTRODUCTION

1. Ronald Reagan, "Just Say No to Clinton's Package," *New York Times,* Op-Ed, August 3, 1993.

CHAPTER 1

1. GDP differs only slightly from GNP (gross national product), the earlier common measure of national product, which includes small amounts of certain receipts from the rest of the world. See *Economic Report of the President* (Washington, D.C.: GPO, 1993), 370.

2. Treasury securities make up approximately 99.5 percent of the gross federal debt. The rest is debt issued by other federal agencies, almost all of which is debt sold to the public by the Tennessee Valley Authority. See Office of Management and Budget, *Analytical Perspectives, Budget of the United States Government, Fiscal Year 1997* (Washington, D.C.: GPO, 1996), 191.

3. Office of Management and Budget, *Analytical Perspectives, Budget of the United States Government, Fiscal Year 1996* (Washington, D.C.: GPO, 1995), 188. The budget also states that "issuing debt to Government accounts does not have any of the economic effects of borrowing from the public. It is an internal transaction between two accounts, both within the Government itself. It does not represent either current transactions of the Government with the public or an estimated amount of future transactions with the public" (188).

4. *Analytical Perspectives, FY96,* 251.

5. Unlike the Social Security and other major "trust funds," the Thrift Savings Fund is not included in the federal budget totals and is classified as a "nonbudget" fund. I was the executive director of the Federal Retirement Thrift Investment Board, which administers the Thrift Savings Fund, from 1986 to 1994.

6. Robert Kuttner, ". . . And the Budget Battle Cry," *Washington Post,* May 22, 1995, A23. © 1995, Washington Post Writers Group. Reprinted with permission.

7. National debt of $5 trillion divided by U.S. population of 260 million.

8. Bill Clinton, *State of the Union Address* (Washington, D.C.: GPO, February 17, 1993). The President misspoke in saying that a $635 billion deficit would be almost 80 percent of gross domestic product (which was approximately $7 trillion in 1995). He apparently meant to say that the *debt* would be 80 percent of GDP.

CHAPTER 2

1. While a portion of the U.S. public debt is held by foreigners, this is not necessarily a burden on future generations of Americans, as explained in chapter 6.

2. The incidence of borrowing—that is, who bears the burden of the interest costs—is discussed in chapter 5.

3. *Economic Report of the President,* 1993, 435.

4. Herbert Stein, "The People vs. the People," *Wall Street Journal,* April 20, 1995, A12.

5. Peter G. Peterson, *Facing Up: How to Rescue the Economy from Crushing Debt and Restore the American Dream* (New York: Simon and Schuster, 1993), 43.

6. *Facing Up,* 59.

7. "House of Debt," *Economist,* April 1–7, 1995, 14.

8. "Annual Message to the Congress on the State of the Union, January 7, 1960," in *Public Papers of the Presidents, Dwight D. Eisenhower 1960–61* (Washington, D.C.: GPO, 1961), 13.

9. Some economists suggested that Eisenhower's statement could be correct under certain assumed economic conditions. An excellent discussion of that minority view appeared in the *American Economic Review* in September 1960 (William G. Bowen, Richard G. Davis, and David H. Kops, "The Public Debt: A Burden on Future Generations") and March 1961 (William Vickrey, Tidor Scitovsky, James R. Elliott, William G. Bowen, Richard G.

Davis, and David H. Kops, "The Burden of the Public Debt"). The standard argument accepted by most economists was perhaps expressed best by Nobel Prize winner Paul A. Samuelson in the following quote from the September 1960 *Review:* "To fight a war now, we must hurl present-day munitions at the enemy; not dollar bills, and not future goods and services" (701).

10. James D. Savage, *Balanced Budgets and American Politics* (Ithaca, N.Y.: Cornell University Press, 1988), 128.

11. Excerpt from House Speaker Newt Gingrich's address to the nation, "All of Us Together . . . Must Totally Remake the Federal Government," *Washington Post,* April 8, 1995, A12.

12. U.S. savings bonds held their value after the war because they were redeemable before maturity at purchase price plus accrued interest, but the value of long-term Treasury marketable securities purchased during the war (and for many years after the war) suffered substantial declines as market interest rates rose after the war. (See discussion of the Treasury 3¼ percent bonds in chapter 8.) This loss of value was not an intergenerational problem; the generation that inherited the depreciated assets also (as taxpayers) inherited a reduced liability to service the national debt.

13. *Analytical Perspectives, FY96,* 110. The Office of Management and Budget presents illustrative operating and capital budgets and states, "The difference between the operating budget deficit and the unified budget deficit is small, reflecting both the relatively small federal investment in new fixed assets and the offsetting effect of depreciation on the existing stock."

14. *Analytical Perspectives, FY96,* 108–114.

15. "A Citizen's Guide to the Federal Budget," in *Budget of the U.S. Government, FY96,* 11.

16. *Budget of the U.S. Government, FY96,* 41, 45.

17. *Analytical Perspectives, FY96,* 108–114.

CHAPTER 3

1. Benjamin M. Friedman, *Day of Reckoning: The Consequences of American Economic Policy* (New York: Random House, 1988), 248.

2. Clinton, *State of the Union Address,* 1993.

3. Peter Brimelow, "Why the Deficit Is the Wrong Number," *Forbes,* March 15, 1993, 79.

4. *Analytical Perspectives, FY97,* 159.

5. U.S. Treasury Department, *The Effect of Deficits on Prices of Financial Assets: Theory and Evidence,* March 1984, 82.

6. Walter B. Wriston, *The Deficit Debate: Critical Crossroads to the Future* (New York: Touche Ross and Co., 1984), 74.

7. Paul Starobin, "Weak Link," *National Journal,* January 29, 1994, 231–234.

8. *Economic Report of the President,* 1993, 474.

CHAPTER 4

1. Abba P. Lerner, "Functional Finance and the Federal Debt," *Social Research* 10 (February 1983): 38–51.

2. Martin A. Armstrong, "The Clinton Crisis," *Wall Street Journal,* April 19, 1995, A14.

3. Office of Management and Budget, *A Vision of Change for America* (Washington, D.C.: February 17, 1993), 127.

4. The average length of the privately held marketable Treasury debt declined from approximately ten years at the end of World War II to a low of two-and-a-half years in 1976 (because of congressional limitations on Treasury's authority to issue long-term securities) and then gradually increased to six years in 1990 before the Clinton administration reduced it to five years by 1996.

5. Interest on the debt will be even more unpredictable, since the Treasury Department has reduced the amount of thirty-year bonds and other long-term security issues and thus relies more on short-term financing at the more volatile short-term interest rates. This is discussed more fully in chapter 10.

6. Board of Governors of the Federal Reserve System, *Federal Reserve Bulletin,* July 1995, A40.

CHAPTER 5

1. U.S. Treasury Department, "Ownership of and Interest Payments on the Public Debt," unpublished study prepared in May 1984 in response to a request from Senator Daniel P. Moynihan (D-N.Y.) to Secretary of the Treasury Donald T. Regan, 17. (Based on my recollection of staff discussions at the time, Senator Moynihan expected the Treasury's statistics to show that the interest on the public debt was regressive, an inequity that he reportedly intended to publicize in the 1984 presidential campaign.)

2. An earlier private study, with a somewhat different approach, concluded that "A comparison of the 1945 federal tax and public debt structures reveal that the progressivity of these two structures is much the same." This statement appeared in an abstract of a doctoral thesis: Donald C. Miller,

"The Transfer Problem: The Relation of the Federal Tax Structure to the Public Debt Structure in 1945" (Ph.D. diss., University of Illinois, 1948, 12; Library of Congress call number HJ 8119.M48).

3. *Ownership of and Interest Payments on the Public Debt,* 13.

4. Fritz Hollings, "Here's a Great Tax," *New York Times,* February 15, 1993, Op-Ed.

5. The National Association of Letter Carriers, "Interest Revisited," *Postal Record,* February, 1994, 13. Reprinted with permission.

6. Mr. Sauber's letter, dated April 25, 1994, details his extensive detective work in tracing the source of the phony statistic. He found that "the original source for the claim that the 10 percent of America's richest families own 85 percent of outstanding Treasury securities was a Washington newsletter of a large industrial union." The union had apparently misinterpreted a passage from William Greider's book on the Federal Reserve, *Secrets of the Temple,* which cited data from an internal Federal Reserve study on the distribution of financial wealth in 1979. Mr. Sauber states:

> First, the Federal Reserve study cited by Greider dealt with *net financial assets* (i.e., assets minus liabilities), not gross assets, much less bonds or even government bonds.
>
> Second, the Fed study focused on the net assets held by *individuals,* excluding what was held by institutions—a fact that Greider made clear in text of his book.

Thus, as Sauber notes, the study excluded the most important purchasers of Treasury securities.

Mr. Sauber concludes, "In short, a quote taken out of context about an outdated study from a book served as the basis for an unjustifiable inference about the ownership of the national debt. This inference gained currency as 'fact' in the nation's labor circles via an unreleased paper by an analyst at a Washington policy shop and ended up in the publications of at least two major unions."

7. The certificates were authorized by the act of February 26, 1879, in denominations of $10 "to bring them within the reach of small investors." U.S. Treasury Department, *The Annual Report of the Secretary of the Treasury on the State of Finances for the Year 1879* (Washington, D.C.: GPO, 1879), xvii.

CHAPTER 6

1. *Analytical Perspectives, FY97,* 197. January 1979 percentage derived from U.S. Treasury Department, *Treasury Bulletin,* June 1979, 79–80.

2. *Analytical Perspectives, FY97,* 196.

3. John M. Berry, "The Whole World on Our Greenback," *Washington Post,* June 9, 1995, C1.

4. In the early 1960s, and again in the late 1970s, the U.S. Treasury issued some relatively small amounts of securities denominated in other currencies, but all the federal debt currently held by foreigners is denominated in dollars. In the early 1980s, the Treasury rejected proposals from Japanese bankers to issue yen-denominated Treasury securities to Japanese investors. Given the volume, liquidity, and universal acceptance of dollar-denominated Treasury securities, it was certainly my view as a Treasury debt manager that it was hardly worthwhile to bother with the marginal amounts of issues that could be sold in other currencies.

5. Alan S. Blinder, *Debt and the Twin Deficits Debate* (Mountain View, Calif.: Mayfield Publishing Co., 1991), 218. Blinder was undoubtedly referring to the power of the Federal Reserve Board to increase the money supply, which would be reflected largely in increased bank deposits rather than in actual increases in the supply of "printed" currency (as discussed in chapter 2).

6. Milton Friedman, "A Deficit That's Good for Us," *Washington Post,* August 8, 1993, C7.

7. Mitchell Pacelle and Steven Lipin, "How Missed Signals and Pride Undid Rockefeller Center," *Wall Street Journal,* May 22, 1995, C1.

8. Mitchell Pacelle, "Japan's U.S. Property Deals: A Poor Report Card," *Wall Street Journal,* June 9, 1995, B1.

9. Milton Freidman, "Why the Twin Deficits Are a Blessing," *Wall Street Journal,* February 14, 1988, A18.

10. Robert L. Heilbroner and Peter L. Bernstein, *The Debt and the Deficit: False Alarms/Real Possibilities* (New York: W. W. Norton and Co., 1989), 33.

11. Clay Chandler and John M. Berry, "Action on Dollar Rejected," *Washington Post,* April 26, 1995, A1.

CHAPTER 7

1. *Analytical Perspectives, FY97,* 198, which also states: "Most Government-sponsored enterprises (GSEs) are financial intermediaries. GSE borrowing (lending) is nevertheless compared with total credit market borrowing (lending) because GSE borrowing (lending) is a proxy for the borrowing (lending) by nonfinancial sectors that is intermediated by GSEs. It assists the ultimate nonfinancial borrower (lender) whose loans are purchased or otherwise financed by GSEs" (198).

2. Office of Management and Budget, *Budget of the United States Government, Fiscal Year 1993* (Washington, D.C.: GPO, 1992), I-300.2.

3. *Analytical Perspectives, FY97*, 198.

4. Cindy Skrzyki, "Departing Fannie Mae Chairman Received $27 Million," *Washington Post*, April 3, 1991, A1.

5. Congressional Budget Office, *Resolving the Thrift Crisis* (Washington, D.C.: GPO, 1993), ix. The higher S&L cost estimates, up to $500 billion, still being claimed by some prominent people are based on the fallacious assumption that the cost is increased by the estimated addition of interest on the Treasury securities issued to finance the $180 billion initial cost to the government under the deposit insurance program. Accepting that assumption (which confuses present value with future value) leads to the nonsensical conclusion that every government (or private) expenditure ultimately costs an infinite amount. Surely, if one spent $180 for an evening on the town one would not say the cost of the evening was $500, or any other amount, even though the $180 could have been invested to grow forever.

6. *Resolving the Thrift Crisis*, ix.

7. Edward J. Kane, *The S&L Insurance Mess: How Did It Happen?* (Washington, D.C.: Urban Institute Press, 1989), 4.

8. *Analytical Perspectives, FY97*, 198.

9. Title V of the Congressional Budget Act of 1974, as amended by section 13201 of the Omnibus Budget Reconciliation Act of 1990.

10. Without this change in budget treatment it seems unlikely that President Clinton would have proposed the recent shift from guaranteed student loans to direct student loans.

11. Public Law 102-550, U.S. Congress (28 October 1992), Section 1355.

12. "Extending the Credit Reform Act to GSEs," Statement no. 131, Shadow Financial Regulatory Committee, Loyola University of Chicago, February 12, 1996, 1–2.

13. *New York Stock Exchange Stock Reports* (New York: Standard & Poor's, 1996), 865T.

14. Ibid., 867.

CHAPTER 8

1. *1995 Annual Report of the Board of Trustees of the Federal Old-Age and Survivors Insurance and Disability Insurance Trust Funds*, House Document 104-57 (Washington, D.C.: GPO, 1995), 181.

2. Ibid., 20.

3. Ibid.

4. It should be noted that a significant labor shortage in the United States would presumably lead to a significant increase in immigrant labor, including professionals and skilled technicians.

5. *1995 Annual Report of Trust Funds,* 23, which states, "if the 75-year actuarial deficit of 2.17 percent under intermediate assumptions were addressed by raising scheduled tax rates by 1.09 percent for employees and employers, each, and by 2.18 percent for the self-employed, then OASDI [Old-Age and Survivors Insurance and Disability Insurance] assets at the beginning of 1995, together with income from payroll taxes, interest, and other sources, would be just sufficient to meet all expenditures for the period and leave a trust fund level at the end of the period equal to about 100 percent of the following year's expenditures."

6. Nancy Ann Jeffrey, " 'Generation X' Starts Saving for Retirement," *Wall Street Journal,* June 15, 1995, C1.

7. Robert M. Ball, "A Proposal for the Advisory Council on Social Security," Unpublished paper, May 10, 1996.

8. Jeff Shear, "Untangling Social Security's Trust Fund," *National Journal,* March 11, 1995, 624.

9. Gingrich, "Remake the Federal Government," A12.

10. Ibid.

11. The Social Security statute actually ensures that the trust fund will get a better deal than private trust funds or other investors in Treasury securities: (1) the fund's investments in short-term Treasury securities earn interest at the Treasury's long-term rates, which are generally much higher than the short-term rates paid by the Treasury to other investors in short-term Treasury securities, and (2) the fund's investments in long-term Treasury securities may be sold back to the Treasury at par value before they reach maturity; thus they are protected from losses to which other investors in long-term Treasury securities are exposed at times of rising market rates of interest.

12. The Social Security trust funds are also authorized to invest in certain securities issued or guaranteed by various federal agencies or government-sponsored enterprises, but currently the funds are invested exclusively in special obligations issued directly to the funds by the U.S. Treasury. See *1995 Annual Report of Trust Funds,* 44.

13. John A. Turner and Daniel J. Beller, eds., *Trends in Pensions* (Washington, D.C.: U.S. Department of Labor, Pension and Welfare Benefits Administration, 1992), 440.

14. Statement of Stephen J. Entin, deputy assistant secretary for Economic Policy, Department of the Treasury, before the Subcommittee on Social Security and Family Policy, Committee on Finance, U.S. Senate, June 30, 1988. These hearings by the Senate Finance Committee were called in part because of concerns at the time that the estimated Social Security trust fund surpluses would be so big that there would not be enough federal debt securities to satisfy the needs of the trust fund and the needs of the private market. This was a needless fear for two reasons: (1) the estimate in 1988 that the Social Security trust fund would peak in 2030 at $12 trillion was a gross overestimate—the current estimate is that the fund will run out of money in 2030—and (2) the gross federal debt in 2030 will be about $37 trillion if the debt continues to increase at the post–World War II average annual rate of 6 percent.

15. Ellen E. Schultz and Charles Gasparino, "Privatizing a Portion of Social Security Could Shower Billions on Mutual Funds," *Wall Street Journal,* February 20, 1996, C1.

16. See note 11.

17. Arthur B. Kennickell and Martha Starr-McCluer, "Changes in Family Finances from 1989 to 1992: Evidence from the Survey of Consumer Finances," *Federal Reserve Bulletin,* Board of Governors of the Federal Reserve System, October 1994, 869.

18. A 1994 poll of adults under age 35 showed 82 percent of respondents supported the privatization option, and 400 to 500 workshop participants at Ross Perot's United We Stand America convention in August 1995 "overwhelmingly supported privatization." Peter J. Ferrara, "The New Politics of Social Security," *Wall Street Journal,* February 14, 1996, A14.

19. Robert Ball and Henry J. Aaron, "Social Security: It *Is* Affordable," *Washington Post,* February 15, 1994, A17.

20. U.S. Treasury Department, *Treasury Bulletin,* November 1982, 55.

CHAPTER 9

1. *Hamlet,* act 1, scene 3.

2. Raju Narisetti, "Figgie's Founder Retires as Chairman and CEO; Interim Successor Named," *Wall Street Journal,* May 19, 1994, B12.

3. Robert H. Schuller and Paul D. Dunn, *The Power of Being Debt Free* (New York: Thomas Nelson Publishers, 1985).

4. The bibliography at the end of this book provides a wide range of both

conservative and liberal views on the national debt in books by prominent economists, businesspeople, clergy, and former government officials.

5. Benjamin M. Freidman, *Day of Reckoning: The Consequences of American Economic Policy* (New York, Random House, 1988), 23.

6. The Budget Bureau, a unit of the Executive Office of the President, was later renamed the Office of Management and Budget.

CHAPTER 10

1. Herbert Stein, *Presidential Economics: The Making of Economic Policy from Roosevelt to Clinton,* 3d ed. (Washington, D.C.: American Enterprise Institute for Public Policy Research, 1994), 345.

2. *Analytical Perspectives, FY96,* 311.

3. *Economic Report of the President* (Washington, D.C.: GPO, 1995), 30.

4. In 1962 I prepared a Treasury staff analysis of the public works acceleration legislation when the bill was pending before Congress. The analysis concluded that the legislation would be counterproductive because, as discussed above, economic recessions are generally too short to be moderated by government spending on capital projects. Thus the economic impact of the authorized projects would come too late and would be procyclical instead of countercyclical. By the time the staff analysis was reviewed at the policy level in the Treasury, political commitments had already been made; so the proposed legislation, though doomed to failure, was enacted into law.

5. Bruce Bartlett, "If It Ain't Broke, Don't Fix It," *Wall Street Journal,* December 2, 1992, A10.

6. Laurence J. Kotlikoff, *Generational Accounting: Knowing Who Pays, and When, for What We Spend* (New York: Free Press, 1992), 246.

7. Steven Pearlstein, "Chicago Economist Awarded Nobel Prize," *Washington Post,* October 11, 1995, C1.

8. "The Annual Report of the Council of Economic Advisers," in *Economic Report of the President,* 1995, 27.

9. *Analytical Perspectives, FY97,* 93.

10. The Participation Sales Act of 1966, a proposal of the Johnson administration, permitted the administration to reduce the budget deficit by employing new consolidated financing techniques to sell substantial amounts of federal agency loans in the private market. This was viewed as a budget gimmick and a primary reason for establishing the President's Commission on Budget Concepts. (Treasury Secretary Henry H. Fowler

was a member of the commission, and I provided staff support for the commission's work on the budget treatment of loans and other financial transactions.)

11. Robert Eisner, *How Real Is the Federal Deficit?* (New York: Free Press, 1986); Robert L. Heilbroner and Peter L. Bernstein, *The Debt and the Deficit* (New York: W. W. Norton and Co., 1989).

12. Heilbroner, *The Debt and the Deficit,* 78.

13. *Analytical Perspectives, FY96,* 7.

14. *Analytical Perspectives, FY96,* 95–118.

15. Alan J. Auerbach, Jagadeesh Gokhale, and Laurence J. Kotlikoff, "Generational Accounts: A Meaningful Alternative to Deficit Accounting," in *Tax Policy and the Economy,* ed. David Bradford (Cambridge, Mass.: MIT Press, 1991), 5: 55–110; Kotlikoff, *Generational Accounting: Knowing Who Pays, and When, for What We Spend.*

16. Office of Management and Budget, "Generational Accounts Presentation," in *Budget of the United States Government, Fiscal Year 1993* (Washington, D.C.: GPO), 3: 7–13; Congressional Budget Office, *Who Pays and When? An Assessment of Generational Accounting* (Washington, D.C.: GPO, 1995). See also Dean Baker, *Robbing the Cradle? A Critical Assessment of Generational Accounting* (Washington, D.C.: Economic Policy Institute, 1995).

17. A similar concern about budget controllability led to the creation in 1967 of the then very successful President's Commission on Budget Concepts, which developed the concept of the currently used unified budget. At the time there was widespread bipartisan support for budget accounting changes to help restore budget credibility and control.

A further revision in federal budget accounting was to be considered by a White House task force established in October 1986 (as reported on the Federal Page of *Washington Post,* October 30, 1986). The primary focus of the task force, which was chaired by the President's counsel, Peter Wallison, was on the question of establishing a capital budget for the government, and a proposal was expected to be included in President Reagan's State of the Union Address in January 1987 (as reported in the lead editorial of the *Washington Post,* October 31, 1986). That effort was aborted, apparently because of the intervention of the Iran-Contra problem.

18. *Analytical Perspectives, FY96,* 215.

19. The deficit reduction fund established by the Clinton administration should not be confused with the *debt* reduction fund established in

1961 (referred to in the preface of this book) to receive voluntary contributions to reduce the public debt. The debt reduction fund is also meaningless in the sense that the voluntary contributions, like other government receipts, automatically reduce the government's need to borrow and thus reduce the public debt. Establishing a separate fund does not change that fiscal reality. Nevertheless, the debt reduction fund is harmless, and it may well help by assuring contributors that their gifts will actually result in debt reduction.

20. The Treasury Direct Book-Entry Securities System permits investors to have direct accounts with the Treasury for their investments in Treasury bills, notes, or bonds. As of August 1995 there were over three million such accounts of which over nine hundred thousand were active (according to the Bureau of the Public Debt of the Treasury Department).

21. Clay Chandler, "Gingrich Vows No Retreat on Debt Ceiling Increase; 'I Don't Care What the Price Is,' Speaker Says," *Washington Post,* September 22, 1995, A13.

22. James K. Glassman, "What Train Wreck," *Washington Post,* October 31, 1995, A13. See also Fred Vogelstein, "Rubin's Warnings on Default Draw Irate Traders to Capitol," *Wall Street Journal,* November 6, 1995, C1.

23. John R. Wilke, "Druckenmiller Shifts Stance on Defaults, Calling GOP Threat 'a Failed Strategy,'" *Wall Street Journal,* January 25, 1996, B9.

24. Ibid.

BIBLIOGRAPHY

Auerbach, Alan J., Jagadeesh Gokhale, and Laurence J. Kotlikoff. "Generational Accounts: A Meaningful Alternative to Deficit Accounting." In *Tax Policy and the Economy.* Vol. 5. Edited by David Bradford, 55–110. Cambridge, Mass.: MIT Press, 1991.

Baker, Dean. *Robbing the Cradle? A Critical Assessment of Generational Accounting.* Washington, D.C.: Economic Policy Institute, 1995.

Brembeck, Cole S. *Congress, Human Nature, and the Federal Debt: Essays on the Political Psychology of Deficit Spending.* New York: Praeger, 1991.

Buchanan, James M. *Public Debt in a Democratic Society.* Washington, D.C.: American Enterprise Institute for Public Policy Research, 1967.

Calleo, David P. *The Bankrupting of America: How the Federal Budget Is Impoverishing the Nation.* New York: William Morrow, 1992.

Committee on Public Debt Policy. *Our National Debt: Its History and Its Meaning Today.* New York: Harcourt Brace, 1949.

Congressional Budget Office. *Who Pays and When? An Assessment of Generational Accounting.* Congress of the United States, November 1995.

Eisner, Robert. *How Real Is the Federal Deficit?* New York: Free Press, 1986.

———. *The Misunderstood Economy: What Counts and How to Count It.* Boston: Harvard Business School Press, 1994.

Ferguson, James M., ed. *Public Debt and Future Generations.* Westport, Conn: Greenwood Press, 1982.

Figgie, Harry E., Jr., with Gerald J. Swanson. *Bankruptcy 1995.* Boston: Little, Brown, 1992.

Fink, Richard H., and Jack C. High, eds. *A Nation in Debt: Economists Debate the Federal Budget Deficit.* Frederick, Md.: University Publications of America, 1987.

Freidman, Benjamin M. *Day of Reckoning: The Consequences of American Economic Policy Under Reagan and After.* New York: Random House, 1988.

"Generational Accounts Presentation," in *Budget of the United States Government, Fiscal Year 1993*, part three, 7–13. Washington, D.C.: GPO, 1994.

Harris, Seymour E. *The National Debt and the New Economics.* New York: McGraw-Hill, 1947.

Heilbroner, Robert L., and Peter L. Bernstein. *The Debt and the Deficit: False Alarms/Real Possibilities.* New York: W. W. Norton, 1989.

Kane, Edward J. *The S&L Insurance Mess: How Did It Happen?* Washington, D.C.: Urban Institute Press, 1989.

Kotlikoff, Laurence J. *Generational Accounting: Knowing Who Pays, and When, for What We Spend.* New York: Free Press, 1992.

Krugman, Paul R. *The Age of Diminished Expectations.* Cambridge, Mass.: MIT Press, 1990.

Malkin, Lawrence. *The National Debt: How America Crashed into a Black Hole and How We Can Crawl Out.* New York: Henry Holt, 1987.

Miller, Donald C. "The Transfer Problem: The Relation of the Federal Tax Structure to the Public Debt Structure in 1945." Ph.D. diss., University of Illinois-Urbana, 1948.

Murphy, Henry C. *The National Debt in War and Transition.* New York: McGraw-Hill, 1950.

Myers, Robert J. *Social Security.* Philadelphia: Pension Research Council, University of Pennsylvania, 1993.

Ortner, Robert. *Voodoo Deficits.* Homewood, Ill.: Dow Jones-Irwin, 1990.

Perot, H. Ross. *Not for Sale at Any Price: How We Can Save America for Our Children.* New York: Hyperion, 1993.

Peters, Harvey W. *America's Coming Bankruptcy: How the Government Is Wrecking Your Dollar.* New Rochelle, N.Y.: Arlington House, 1973.

Peterson, Peter G. *Facing Up: How to Rescue the Economy from Crushing Debt & Restore the American Dream.* New York: Simon & Schuster, 1993.

Rock, James M., ed. *Debt and the Twin Deficits Debate.* Mountain View, Calif.: Mayfield, 1991.

Savage, James D. *Balanced Budgets and American Politics.* Ithaca: Cornell University Press, 1988.

Schuller, Robert H., and Paul D. Dunn. *The Power of Being Debt Free: How Eliminating the National Debt Could Radically Improve Your Standard of Living.* New York: Thomas Nelson Publishers, 1985.

Sennholz, Hans F. *Debts and Deficits.* Spring Mills, Pa.: Libertarian Press, 1987.

Steadman, Charles W. *The National Debt Conclusion: Establishing the Debt Repayment Plan.* Westport, Conn.: Praeger, 1993.

Third Millennium. *Third Millennium Declaration.* New York: Third Millennium, 1993.

U.S. House. *Annual Report of the Board of Trustees of the Federal Old-Age and Survivors Insurance and Disability Insurance Trust Funds.* 104–57. Washington, D.C.: GPO, 1995.

INDEX

ABOUT THE AUTHOR

Francis X. Cavanaugh is a writer and public finance consultant in Washington, D.C. He retired from government work in 1994 after forty-two years. From 1986 to 1994, Mr. Cavanaugh was the first executive director and chief executive officer of the Federal Retirement Thrift Investment Board, an independent financial agency established by Congress to administer the Thrift Savings Plan, a retirement plan for government employees.

He served in the U.S. Department of the Treasury from 1954 to 1986 as an economist and as a senior career executive responsible for advice on the management of the public debt. He was the director of the Treasury's Office of Government Finance and Market Analysis, and secretary and chief operating officer of the Federal Financing Bank.

Mr. Cavanaugh received the President's Award for Distinguished Federal Civilian Service from President Reagan. He also received the Presidential Rank Award of Distinguished Executive in the Senior Executive Service from three presidents—Jimmy Carter, Ronald Reagan, and George Bush.